The Insiders' Guide to BPM
7 Steps to Process Mastery

The Insiders' Guide to BPM

7 Steps to Process Mastery

Terry Schurter

with
Peter Fingar

Meghan-Kiffer Press
Innovation at the Intersection of Business and Technology
Tampa, Florida, USA
www.mkpress.com

Publisher's Cataloging-in-Publication Data

Schurter, Terry
The Insiders' Guide to BPM: 7 Steps to Process Mastery / Terry Schurter, Peter
Fingar - 1st ed.
p. cm.
  Includes index.
  ISBN10: 0-929652-09-6   ISBN13: 978-0-929652-09-2
    1. Management 2. Technological innovation. 3. Diffusion of innovations.
  4. Globalization—Economic aspects. 5. Information technology. 6. Informa-
  tion Society. 7. Organizational change. I. Schurter, Terry. II. Title

HM48.S75 2009   2009937427
303.48'33–dc22   CIP

Book's Web site: www.mkpress.com

Published by Meghan-Kiffer Press
310 East Fern Street — Suite G
Tampa, FL 33604 USA

Meghan-Kiffer books are available at special quantity discounts for corporate
education and training use. For more information write Special Sales, Meghan-Kiffer
Press, Suite G, 310 East Fern Street, Tampa, Florida 33604 or call (813) 251-5531

Meghan-Kiffer Press
USA

Printed in the United States of America. SAN 249-7980
MK Printing 10 9 8 7 6 5 4 3 2 1

About This Book

BPM big wins have been limited to a small cadre
of process masters... but not anymore.
Now everyone is just 7 steps away from process mastery.

We've all heard those stories of BPM success that influenced the bottom line and increased revenues. We've all heard those compelling cases of 50%, 60% even 70+% reductions in process cost with hard ROI payback in 12 months or less. We have heard them and they are very compelling.

Yet it seems that for many of us, those kinds of results remain elusive. Why is that? Perhaps it is because no one has taken the time to distill the essence, in simple terms, of just how to achieve such results. And that is what this book is intended to do.

This book draws out the 7 steps that can help you master your processes, regardless of what *mastering* means to you. This book is your insiders' guide to making BPM work for you. BPM can make a big difference for almost any business goal. BPM can make a difference with almost any process. Everyone can be successful with BPM. But we also know that process mastery has, to date, remained an unfulfilled promise for far too many organizations.

Whether you're seeking the insights to consistently achieve goals with BPM, looking to move yourself from moderate success to big wins, or wanting to keep hitting those process home runs, this book is for you.

Preface

For over a decade, Peter Fingar and I have contributed to thought leadership on Business Process Management (BPM) beginning with Peter's *Real Time Enterprise* and *Business Process Management: The Third Wave*. Then on to *Customer Expectation Management: Success Without Exception* and the role of IT in BPM with *IT Doesn't Matter: Business Processes Do*. We've even explored the international effects of process with *Extreme Competition* and *In Search of BPM Excellence*.

Now, in collaboration with Peter, I am doing something different – reaching down deep into a decade's experience with BPM to unlock what has remained hidden for many people seeking to improve their organizations with process. In this book I have distilled the seven steps individuals and organizations can take to achieve success with their process endeavors. The challenge this book addresses is the gap between the few who experience phenomenal success with BPM and the many who struggle to achieve modest goals, and for whom the big wins seem all too elusive.

The seven steps to mastering your processes are geared to help you join the ranks of the process masters who are driving success in everything they do.

Terry Schurter

October 2009

Foreword by David Mitchell

We are presented with many challenges in successfully operating our organizations. Sometimes those challenges are reflected in our financials (as commercial organizations) and other times they stem from the services we provide as governmental or non-profit agencies. The economic challenges we have been facing for some time now certainly increase our awareness of these challenges, forcing us to sharpen our perceptions and take actions that directly address these challenges—now.

Here at Global360, we are investing our energies into products and services that directly address these challenges by changing how work gets done. Only by changing how we do work can we achieve productivity, efficiency and financial goals that lie outside of our grasp today. Reaching our goals rests squarely in the work we do and how we do it. It is our responsibility to change that for the better.

The most important observation I can share with you is that it is us, the people in our organizations, that either meet those challenges... or don't. And we can meet these challenges. We can change how we do work. We can align and optimize our organizations to deliver against almost any challenge. We just have to do it.

But it's also true that we often don't know how to tackle this challenge. We struggle to get started, we struggle to drive our way to our goal, and we often find that we come up short of what we hoped to gain. To help you address these challenges you have this book—The Insider's Guide to Business Process Management. I recommend you read it to help you sharpen your skills in achieving your goals.

You are also invited to visit us at Global360 to see what we are doing to pave the road to process success. We may not have all of the answers, but we are certainly challenging the status quo and in doing so, finding new ways to increase the success of our customers.

I hope you take the time to stop by and see how we are changing how work gets done.

Regards,

David Mitchell

CEO Global360
www.global360.com

A special thanks to the following people, without whom this book could not be...

Ray Baron
Nathaniel Palmer
Christy Schurter
Jennifer Troxell
Debbie Rosen
Alex Morse
Stephen Phillips
Michael zur Muehlen
Jan Recker
David Kammerdeiner
David McDonald

and Meghan-Kiffer Press.

Contents

The Baseline: Perspectives on Business Process Management

We can chart our future clearly and wisely
only when we know the path which has led to the present.
—Adlai E. Stevenson

Before we describe possible futures, let's quickly reflect on the past and present of Business Process Management (BPM). BPM has its roots in the management practices of Business Process Reengineering (BPR) that emerged in the early 1990's in response to the Japanese companies that were out competing U.S. firms. It all began when quality management gurus Edwards Deming and Joseph Juran worked in Japan after World War II and introduced the notion that quality improvement was about process improvement.

Then, in the early 1990's process kicked into high gear with the advent of Business Process Reengineering (BPR). The BPR movement gained widespread recognition in response to the 1993 book by Michael Hammer and James Champy, *Reengineer-*

ing the Corporation: A Manifesto for Business Revolution. If you are unfamiliar with the term BPR, perhaps you'll no doubt recognize its associated term, "downsizing." At its core, BPR was a radical approach to tearing down departmental silos inside an enterprise and streamlining the business processes that crossed functional departments. Taken to extreme, some companies embraced radical engineering, eliminating scores of departmental mid-managers (gatekeepers) and workers viewed as redundant through the BPR lens. Where Hammer and Champy had intended streamlining and silo elimination, departmental disconnects and redundancies became the common targets of most BPR initiatives. In fact, some companies downsized to the point of anemia, and learned the bitter lessons that a firm cannot command market share simply by saving on costs. Both Hammer and Champy wrote apologies for what they had unleashed with their theories—turns out they didn't really mean for companies to downsize themselves to the point of anemia.

To implement reengineering management practices, in actuality, many companies "reengineered" their processes by installing Enterprise Resource Planning (ERP) application software. It was a grueling and expensive task to configure ERP applications and it wasn't untypical that consultant fees were larger than the software costs. But the real pitfall was that even though processes were malleable while being configured into ERP applications, once implemented those very processes were "cast in concrete." That is the nature of ERP. And that would be okay, except for the fact that the only constant in business is change! Even before many ERP installations were complete, the business was demanding business process change.

———

Fast forward to 2003, and Smith and Fingar's book, *Business Process Management: The Third Wave*, the seminal book on BPM versus BPR: "If end-to-end business processes are the focus of internal and cross-company integration, why not deal directly with the 'business process, as application' instead of 'data' and 'applications?' Because business processes can no longer be cast in concrete the way they are in today's applications, the 'business process' must supersede the 'application' as a means of packaging software. In addition, companies must leverage existing IT investments as they build new process-aware information systems that understand the enterprise process design right across the value chain. Companies are demanding a breakthrough that shifts the locus of automation from the affairs of IT to the affairs of the business. They want to shift their efforts from further automating integration to make up for the limitations of IT, and move on to managing business processes. That breakthrough is the methodology of BPM and its technology engine—the business process management system (BPMS)."

BPM wasn't a big bang, rip-and-replace proposition as was BPR. BPM was seen as a new foundation to realize process innovation and manage incremental process improvement as compared to BPR that was focused on one-time, big-bang projects. Further, BPM took into account the perspective of people, a perspective that was lacking in a majority of BPR initiatives (even though this was not the intent of BPR thought leaders such as Hammer and Champy).

Over the last decade or so a number of software vendors have equated BPM to being, essentially, just *workflow*. Yet workflow software was in use as far back as the early 1980's and was most certainly part of software development even before then. Workflow is the concept of using a routing mechanism to create ordered sequences. Some workflow engines include the concept of branching, meaning that different paths can be taken through the workflow model. But the essence of workflow is based on simple sequences with each step in a sequence existing in relative isolation.

With the advent of Business Process Management Systems (BPMS) to support the concept of workflow *processes*, many improvements have been made to traditional workflow systems. For example *intelligent* work routing represents work that can be directed through a more complex and versatile process model based on complex business rules and real-time events. In this way, work items can be routed to specific people or specific activities based on the intelligence that is built into the workflow model itself.

Workflow-style BPM systems now offer many other features and functions beyond traditional workflow orchestration such as multiple perspectives on process modeling, case handling, exception routing, complex business rule-set management, work analysis, document management, integration capabilities and many more. There are also workflow-style BPM systems that focus solely on modeling and simulation, often used by analysts and enterprise architects.

Early entrants into the BPMS market created new workflow tools that often required little code development to express business processes dependent heavily on human touch points. The belief within the early BPMS community was that by providing *business users* with a simple set of tools, these business users would model workflow-centric processes directly; improving the efficiency and quality of business operations. Considering that these same business users are the people responsible for day-to-day process operation the approach seemed to hold much merit, even to the point of tapping a wealth of untapped improvement opportunities lying dormant in our organizations. This was particularly true where little technology was in place, and where consistency in the process was poor at best. Early case studies that arose from using a BPMS for these workflow-style processes were compelling examples of what might be gained by deploying this kind of software.

However, most *business users* did not pick up on the opportunity to be *directly* involved in the modeling of processes, causing BPMS vendors to fall short of critical market mass with this approach. The BPMS market growth was still strong, though not as strong as many had predicted, but it began to change. The BPMS market started shifting its focus to technologists, relegating the business user perspective to a marketing strategy, not a product strategy. This was the turning point for a market that was struggling, converting it to one of strong growth—enough so to gain the attention of larger software vendors. That led to numerous acquisitions of smaller "pure-play" BPM software firms by larger software vendors. These changes drove BPMS products into more of an Information Technology focus, further distancing BPM from its original business focus. The result is a healthy software market experiencing continued strong growth with a strong undercurrent of despair.

An anonymous investor in one of the early BPMS companies (that has since been acquired) really tells the BPMS story. "We saw that BPM had an opportunity to solve a fundamental business challenge. We thought it was that once-in-a-lifetime opportunity. It was a good investment, but it didn't really change anything. You know, change how businesses operate, adapt, and grow. Even change the economics of business. We knew it was close to that. But something was missing. It didn't solve the problem. The challenge is still there."

Market Split: Integration versus Workflow

Between acquisitions, product development and repositioning of existing BPMS products, a fundamental shift started to take place. The shift was to use the BPMS concept to solve a different problem, the development of *automated* business processes that require little or no human intervention. This new emphasis was focused primarily on *straight-thru* IT automation—behind the scenes, back office handling of processes with little, if any, human intervention. The split soon became reflected in the language of the market, with *integration-centric* BPM and *workflow-centric* BPM identified as separate classes of BPMS products.

Workflow-centric processes involve multiple stakeholders and require changing the behavior of people in the organization—a task that can be quite difficult to achieve. Conversely, integration-centric processes are essentially an IT function, and as such are confined to those with a technical mindset who already have significant domain knowledge regarding the problems to be solved. In fact, integration-centric BPM is often considered the next iteration of enterprise application integration (EAI) along with the newly minted Web-oriented Service-Oriented Architecture (SOA.)

Cost reduction is perhaps the most targeted benefit of BPM systems with case studies validating 20%, 30% and even 50+% reductions in the operating cost of a given process. Cost reduction with BPM systems is achieved through a mixture of automation, process streamlining, error reduction, elimination of duplicity, and better control over processes at both the work level (people doing work in the process) and management level (those overseeing and balancing demands against resources).

However, cost reduction remains highly unpredictable in actual practice and is most often limited to workflow-centric processes. Integration-centric BPM offers its value more in speeding up IT response to change requirements, something that has slipped out of our grasp in many cases. It's not uncommon for existing IT complexity to push simple business change requests out three to nine months.

Even with workflow-centric processes, many organizations are struggling to achieve demonstrable gains. Yet business innovation and business transformation—two of the challenges early investors thought BPM would solve— can far outweigh cost reduction as BPM's ultimate benefit.

Process Improvement by Methodology

When the focus moves to changing "how work gets done" in the organization, the discussion immediately moves away from software into the arena of management methods and business practice. This is the domain of various process improvement methodologies such as Six Sigma, Lean, TQM, CEM, and Change Management. This is why Six Sigma and Lean have quickly been crossed over into the BPM market as these are improvement methods or philosophies that are intended to help organizations optimize existing operations.

On the other hand, methods such as Six Sigma have fallen short of their perceived value propositions. Even 3M, the poster child of Six Sigma, has moved away from the approach in favor of new methods that focus on innovation more than cost reduction. Like cost reduction achieved through the use of BPM systems, process improvements through the application of specific management methodologies sport a number of compelling case studies that highlight the opportunity—but while consistently achieving improvement, breakout results remain elusive overall.

Six Sigma, Lean, and TQM are based on incrementally improving a process rather than challenging the process against how it might be shaped to achieve breakthrough benefits. The reason these approaches are so limited is that their philosophical approach accepts the basic process shape (the AS IS model) as valid, seeking to refine the process within the current constrained model of most processes. In reality, many processes are not currently based on a process model aimed at innovating how work *should* or *could* get done. Therefore, they are not properly aligned with achieving the desired outcome of the organization—that is, moving beyond the current status quo.

Applying techniques or methodologies focused on incremental improvement can yield a process that is streamlined against the wrong outcome. A number of experienced insiders have now come to describe this situation as *making the same mistakes, only faster.* Paving cow paths, anyone?

Industry Trends and Common Practice

The benefits organizations seek to derive from BPM cover a broad range of specific agendas such as cost reduction, service improvement, productivity, error reduction, compliance, oversight, and business transformation. The motivations for using BPM as a management philosophy and as a technology vary widely and have significant correlations to the *other BPM* (Business *Performance* Management) that focuses on business performance across the enterprise. Current economic conditions have led many organizations to increase their focus on Business Performance Management initiatives.

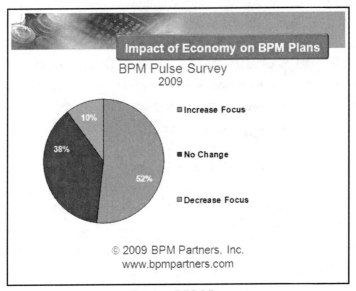

Courtesy BPM Partners

Illustrating this, the BPM Partners' 2009 BPM Pulse Survey showed that economic conditions have indeed had a dramatic impact on the importance of performance improvement.

With over 50% of the 750+ respondents indicating an increased interest in directly managing performance, it's clear that performance is high on corporate agendas.

From the report written by Nathanial Palmer in 2006 and published by BPTrends in January 2007 (A Survey of Business

Process Initiatives) we can see that organizations use BPM systems for a variety of reasons. From this study it is also clear that the top priority is the improvement of existing processes.

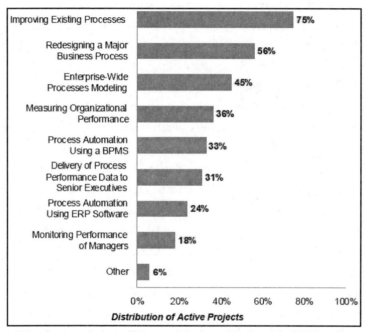

Distribution of Active Projects, Nathaniel Palmer & BPTrends

Although such survey results certainly make sense, the challenge for most people isn't figuring out what *should* be done; it is really a question of *how* to achieve improvement. That, of course, is the purpose of this book – to provide the *how*.

Considering that there is every indication of a perceived need to implement BPM to improve some aspect of organizational performance, then what are the results of such observations? Is it a given that using BPM will produce the desired outcome? Not likely.

In a research report by Gartner, the analyst firm states that over half of the BPM programs undertaken by organizations will fail over a period of two years because they are implemented without the necessary supporting disciplines. This is further borne out by the ongoing debates over process modeling approaches and standards that continue to rage unchecked as various pundits, researchers, analysts, technologists and professors join the fray.

Another interesting observation on the limitations of achieving success with BPM comes from a research firm, the Aberdeen Group. Surveying 160 business and IT professionals, Aberdeen found that: "Part of the [BPM] solution is technical, but another part is organizational, and this is where many companies stumble. It takes highly capable BPM products, a willingness to take a hard look at business processes to succeed, and organizational maturity."

This emphasis on people is further supported with the results of an independent survey with participants of a recent Gartner BPM conference. In this survey, 781 business and technology analysts, managers and executives were polled with some of the questions in the survey digging into unexplored, or perhaps it is more accurate to say studiously ignored, areas of BPM. When asked how often end users of software applications "design their own workarounds," due to how difficult it is for them to use these applications, 48% of respondents indicated this happened "often" and 37% indicated it happened "occasionally."

That means that 85% of end users find the process design, user interface or user experience of BPM systems sufficiently inappropriate for their needs that they take the concerted effort to create their own *process workarounds* to get work done.

Interesting, isn't it? We seek to improve our processes, yet we often produce processes that are unwieldy, non-intuitive or even inappropriate for the people who are responsible for actually doing the work on a daily basis. How can we expect to achieve performance, productivity or cost reduction targets when the process doesn't conform to the reality of getting work done? Of course we shouldn't have such expectations, yet the majority of BPM projects fail to address the critical people factor.

Consider the case where BPM was employed in an assembly plant of a high volume manufacturer. While the process had been run through extensive validation and even simulation (software simulation) to ensure the process would perform as intended, that is not at all what really happened. On-floor terminals provided custom build instructions, but while the correct information was indeed presented; layout, terminology, and sequencing did not reflect current practices and behaviors. People didn't know what to do with the new system and with production pressures mounting they started implementing a variety of ineffective manual workarounds, quickly turning the assembly line into chaos. The new system was pulled and operations reverted to the old way of doing work. The process team then went back to work to wrestle with the need to make the process relevant to the workers of the assemble line—duh!

From this real life example, we can observe that the relevance of a BPM deployment on how people *really* do work is what counts. As we continue our insiders' tour of BPM, we will uncover and provide the guidance to address the reasons why BPM projects often fail to meet expectations. It's obvious to us that BPM can be a major lever for improving any organization on numerous fronts. It is also obvious that far too many people don't know how to do that, which is why we have distilled seven steps that people can take to help make BPM deliver business results.

Before we delve into those specifics there remains one more piece of background that needs to be considered: the concept of *perspectives on process*. In the next section we will explore that concept and how it can be used to break past the challenges that are limiting companies' success with BPM.

Perspectives on Process

It was six men of Indostan
To learning much inclined,
Who went to see the Elephant
(Though all of them were blind),
That each by observation
Might satisfy his mind... —John Godfrey Saxe

By perspectives, we refer to the views of a given business process held by different groups of people and the roles they play in those processes. Though perhaps a little trite, the story of the blind men and the elephant can indeed be instructive for us. The story dates back at least to the 13th century and describes a situation where the blind men each feel a different part of the elephant, resulting in beliefs of *what an elephant is* that are dramatically different from each other.

Blind monks examining an elephant by Hanabusa Itchō

In John Godfrey Saxe's version of the story each blind man describes his impression of the elephant. Thus we find the elephant described as a wall, a snake, a spear, a tree, a fan and a rope. Each of these observations comes from a specific perspective, and while all of them are *true* within the confines of the individual perspective they represent, they do not describe the elephant. Even when all of these perspectives are combined into one compound description, that description falls short.

Business processes exist in much the same way. There are a number of perspectives that people have for a particular process, and each of those perspectives represents only a portion of the process—not the whole. Would it surprise you to find that just like *the learned men from Indostan*, the role or responsibility each person has in "process" is likely to define, or shape, how they see process? It shouldn't because that is exactly what happens. Our context gives us an individual perspective on the organization that is not holistic. People are influenced heavily by their context – far more than we realize in BPM projects even if we have studied cognitive science. Most of us have not.

We must have a common understanding of process and we must understand that other people's perspectives differ. We also must understand enough about those other perspectives so that we can recognize why they are important to the central idea of process management.

Common understanding must be just that – common. That means we cannot impose any need to understand terms, perspectives or mindsets on the conversation that must occur at the highest level of process description. That means no need for translation – none.

To reinforce further the challenge of different perspectives, we can look at an optical illusion that does a good job of showing us how perspectives can really shape understanding.

Optical Illusion – Observational Perspectives
Courtesy David McDonald (david.mac@skynet.be)

In this image, depending on the point of observation, we are on a balcony looking down or we are on a terrace looking up. The image of the terrace or balcony gives a vivid symbolic representation of the challenge we face in relating to the observational points of view between those working on process as a structure and those performing work within the process. While both references are clearly focused on the same thing (in our case, a process), the observational points completely change our perception of the common, or shared, reference.

For process, we should take this illusion and apply it to how we understand process and as a reminder of how each person involved with a process is likely to *see* the process far differently than we do.

Fortunately, we really don't have to understand process from all perspectives at the same time. We can get to where we want to go by knowing what perspectives exist, and then accounting for them in our approach. While this is not one of the seven steps to mastering our processes, it is the foundation we use to identify those steps. It guides both our actions and our understanding to make our results more successful Now let's explore the perspectives that exist for process by looking at the whole *elephant* rather than just a leg, a nose, an ear or a tail.

Someone Needs to...

From conception to operation, then on to adaptation, process success is determined by the ability of people to interact with processes in a simple, personal and meaningful way.

While many of these needs remain largely unmet, someone, some person, somebody, still has to:

- Identify what process will be improved, and determine the Key Performance Indicators (KPIs) that accurately reflect the desired outcome of the process.
- Design the process model by figuring out what tasks must be performed, what dependencies exist and how work will *flow* through the process.
- Build an executable process model, automating tasks and activities where possible, integrating with other systems and embedding active documents where needed.
- Perform the tasks and activities of the process, deal with the daily nuances that occur, and adapt to ad hoc requirements that often involve other people and resources to *get the job done.*
- Oversee process operations; make strategic decisions to adjust resources to work demand, staff availability, and priority of assignments.
- Review process performance, develop a line-of-sight into trends and patterns, predict emerging challenges and identify new opportunities for improvement.
- Provide strategic oversight, make strategic decisions and *piece together* the big picture to ensure the organization remains on track to achieve goals and shareholder value.

All of these *somebodies* contribute process success. Furthermore, each of these *somebodies* is one or more people with their own preferences, behaviors, organizational style and approaches to carrying out work. By supporting these varying roles and activities in the process approach, and including the ability for people in the process to personalize their process experience, process success can be achieved in a predictable and consistent manner. In many ways this is the real underlying challenge we face. We can, however, take these things into account with the seven steps in this book. First though, we will organize various perspectives into groups with similar characteristics—what we call affinity groups.

Affinity Groups:
Builders, Participants and Managers

The three affinity groups that are easiest to break out can be labeled builders, participants and managers. These groups exhibit similar characteristics and common purpose or experience with respect to their role in a given process.

Builders are involved in determining what will be done, how, when and why. They set the stage for process operation, as well as the shaping of the process to achieve desired outcomes. The builder's view of process is a construction view, and thus it is usually viewed as a *project*.

Participants do the actual work in the process, handling the day-to-day tasks and activities that are part of each process constructed by the builders. It is important to note that participants have by far the most *face-time* with the process; after all the participants are *living* in the process every day. They are the ones likely to feel the pain, and to be motivated to find ways to *work around* inefficient or inappropriate process designs.

Affinity Groups in Process

From the perspective of its participants, a poorly constructed process will result in ongoing frustration and anxiety. Can you imagine how you would feel if your house was designed or built in a way that just did not fit your needs? What if the doors weren't tall enough and you had to stoop to enter? Can you imagine how it would feel to have the kitchen cabinets in one room in the front of the house, with kitchen appliances in the back? How would you feel if the master bedroom faced east with a sweeping set of windows that usher the rising sun into your room—but you sleep late in the mornings? That might significantly impact your living experience. A house often looks fine until we start living in it – that's when we discover it doesn't really meet our needs.

You've probably experienced this to some degree (hopefully not to the extreme) because in most cases builders miss a lot of things that matter to participants. Sometimes, of course, builders *miss* things due to design constraints, resources available and other limitations. The point is that what process builders build directly influences the comfort and convenience (or lack thereof) experienced by participants that do the work.

Managers' process roles are to provide oversight, guidance, leadership and direction. Managers must view process as an aggregate of work for a given range or domain of the organization. Managers make critical observations that result in changing participants' focus and work prioritization to ensure that overall outcomes are met in a desired manner. The management view is a *big picture* perspective of the relationship between demand, resources, outcomes and context. This view is needed to support effective decision-making.

An analogy of the relationships between the affinity groups involved in process can help to build a complete 360-degree view of process. Let's think of processes in a transportation setting. Builders would build the roads, participants would drive vehicles and managers would provide the oversight and control to keep traffic flowing smoothly. While each role in the analogy represents a fundamentally difference perspective, they combine to produce a desired outcome. Success in the transportation analogy requires well designed infrastructure (roads, process model), drivers to handle the actual work of driving vehicles (process work), and managers to orchestrate overall flow patterns (prioritization, exception routing, strategic planning). Without all of these elements, working in harmony, the transportation analogy cannot be optimized to achieve a desired outcome.

Builders, participants and managers have defined roles within the overall perspective of process, yet they are dependent on each other to achieve overall process success. The interrelationships among builders, participants and managers must be molded into a synergistic view if the potential value of a process is to be realized.

Process Relationships to Technology

Another way to view the relationship of these affinity groups to each other is by their relationship to supporting technology. As shown in the figure below, at the highest level of the software infrastructure we find Document Management, Case Management and Process Management. It's at this level where technology interfaces with the people involved in process work. These interfaces are what most people (other than some of the builders) see and think of as process software.

Of course there are other essential technology layers that aren't seen by everyone. Some of these include business and integration services, storage, and data access as well as some of our old friends, those legacy applications that were the *cutting edge technologies of the time* when we first plugged them into our technology stack.

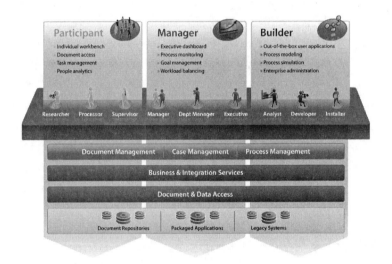

Common Software Infrastructure for Process

The software infrastructure for process must deal with multiple affinity groups and multiple technology layers that have direct and indirect relationships to one another. Process success relies on all of these process elements as well as (and even more so) their relationships to one another.

Builders – Setting the Landscape

Call them process owners, architects, business analysts, process specialists, line-of-business owners, or IT professionals. Whatever the job title may be, someone makes the decisions about what processes are going to be targeted for improvement, why and what results the improved process should achieve. These people are process builders, and their role involves setting the stage for process improvement projects. They do this by identifying improvement opportunities, building business cases, crafting process KPIs, and preparing the overall process plan.

However, sometimes it's not easy to identify process improvement opportunities, or to determine how to leverage an opportunity to create organizational success. Many opportunities stem from an existing undesirable process outcome, and while this undesirable outcome may be understood, it can be challenging to determine how to improve the process. In other cases, it's not even obvious where the best opportunities lie. For many BPM initiatives, failure at this initial opportunity discovery step is an immediate barrier to achieving success. For others, the difficulty in navigating through the challenges in identifying and justifying process improvement on business-critical processes causes organizations to detour toward less critical processes (such as internal support processes or internal policy management). When this happens, tacit agreement is made to leave the game-changing opportunity *off the table* because that higher-value opportunity is just too challenging for builders to adequately address.

With that said, and for BPM to realize its true potential, builders must be able to identify high-value process opportunities, and be able to build the supporting business cases behind them. If builders are not able to address significant challenges, then BPM has little chance of realizing more than a fraction of the potential process improvement or innovation.

Participants – Personalization

Based on what the builders build, participants in the process do the work. They carry out tasks and activities, and provide the feedback needed for analysis and incremental optimization. Participants can include employees in a number of roles such as operational staff and support personal, but there are also participants outside the organization, including business partners and customers.

Regardless of who the participants are, they need a way to interact with a process that is specifically relevant to their roles, contexts and responsibilities. For process success to be realized, processes cannot burden participants with the onerous challenge of *figuring out* process interfaces and how to use them to accomplish their tasks.

The participant group has a common performance-based characteristic that differs significantly from that of builders. Where builders have more of a project-based perspective, participants live in a world of daily workloads. Their needs are clear. Process success demands that participants be given an interface into the process that aligns directly with their wants, needs and contexts, an interface that intuitively makes their work easier. Anything less and they will be forced to find their own ways to get their work done, and that takes them *outside* of the designed process.

Yet the approach to participant interfaces remains fundamentally flawed in many BPM initiatives. Too often BPM software addresses participant interfaces from the perspective of software, not from that of the participants. While good practice and attractive user interface (UI) design elements may be in place, ergonomic, behavioral and contextual needs are often overlooked. The typical approach is *one size fits all*, with a prevailing attitude that as long as what is needed to perform the work of the process is available, that is *good enough*. In reality, many user interfaces are not good and certainly not enough.

To be effective in their work, process participants need interfaces that are based on behavioral, contextual and ergonomic analysis. Furthermore, process participants must be able to personalize their process experience, giving them the ability to adjust their *relationship* with the process to suit their individual needs. Consider the driver of an automobile, where the functions of the seat, mirrors and steering wheel do not change from driver to driver, but adjustments to these functional aspects of the automobile interface are highly desired and beneficial to individual drivers.

Process participants need this same flexibility to personalize their interaction with a given process. If participants are not provided with personalized supported in the work they do, then process success will be compromised. Personalization is the first ingredient required to empower process participant success. The next ingredient involves collaboration.

Process Participants – Collaboration

Process participants also require capabilities to deal with the many variances that occur when performing the work of a process. Process participants must deal with contextual nuances, exceptions, ad hoc requirements and many other variables that are part of the environment involved in performing the work of a process. They must work with teammates, other departments and with customers. Their work often requires finding information and getting answers from a variety of internal and external sources.

In the initial design phase of a process improvement project, it is impossible to identify all of the challenges process participants will face, so a combination of flexibility and collaboration capability is needed.

Collaboration must provide the means for process participants to easily seek expert knowledge, validation, assistance, and creative input, and to deal with ad hoc requirements. Such collaboration capabilities form the cornerstone of effectively dealing with process variances.

But this is not a case of just providing collaborative technologies. The challenge with process work is that process participants need collaborative support *integrated* into the context of a process. While there are many ways to provide collaborative support for workers in general, only by providing process-aware collaboration can we actually make this part of the participant experience simpler and more productive. In short, integrated collaboration capabilities are needed to support how process participants actually do the work they do in the real world full of exceptions and unique cases.

Process Participants – Adaptation

Finally, it's extremely important for process participants to capture the sources of variances; the discussions that are held to address them; and the actions taken to resolve them. By capturing these real-world process experiences, process feedback is available to help uncover new areas of process improvement and refinement. Process participant feedback is vital to increasing process performance and improving process quality.

Why do we care so much about adaptation? In many respects, processes are best viewed as *living entities* that are subject to ongoing change pressures from internal and external forces. The ability to capture process feedback, without requiring process participants to engage in a separate feedback process, is an essential part of maintaining process efficiency and relevancy over time.

More traditional BPM approaches conduct lagging analysis, periodic process re-analysis or impose a separate feedback process. Such approaches seek to fix things when they are broken. The key is capturing feedback on changing work patterns as exceptions and variances occur, and before things are broken. This real-time feedback is the only viable means to ensure that processes are adaptive throughout their complete life cycles. In short, processes should be built to adapt to an ever-changing work environment.

Managers – Providing Oversight, Direction and Leadership

Where builders set the stage for processes and participants perform the work in processes, managers must have visibility into aggregate results of living processes. Such transparency is required for managers to provide oversight, direction and leadership. Process managers may be tasked with repurposing resources to meet demand patterns that can often vary substantially. Examples of such demand fluctuations include:

1. A planned event induces a sales surge (product launch, sales promotion).
2. An unplanned event triggers a support influx (act of nature, insurance claims).
3. A reduction in available staff (an influenza outbreak).

These examples are a few of the many factors that can cause process load and resources to fluctuate. One of the roles of the process manager is to balance resources versus demand in the best way possible to meet desired performance outcomes.

At other times managers must look at higher-level trends to

manage shareholder value or make the strategic decisions that lead to continuing success. Further, managers at all levels are often seeking to uncover new opportunities for business improvement and strategic initiatives.

Managers - Information is Often Captured but Rarely Relevant

While the information needed to perform management functions is often captured in computer systems: that information is rarely presented in a form that is easy to consume. Stated another way, information is available but not in a form that makes it easy for managers to enact oversight, make decisions and provide leadership. Information or data, in and of itself, is not enough. Only when relevant information is presented in a way that is intuitive and aggregated at the right level can managers consistently make good decisions. Left without such views into the business, managers are challenged to provide reality-based decisions.

Even where management decision-making abilities are stellar, ineffective decisions are common. Irrelevant, difficult to decipher or improper sets of the information needed to properly support the decision-making process cripples even the best managers. For BPM to be successful, managers must be empowered to spend their time, energy and intellectual capacity on solving actual problems and taking advantage of new opportunities as they appear on the radar – rather than spending their time deciphering cryptic information and data.

Successful BPM Embraces all of the People in Process

Process mastery must embrace the perspectives of all three affinity groups involved in process work. Giving them their unique views into the overall process can result in business performance that meets or exceeds expectations. There are no painful surprises when each of the roles in process work is taken fully into account. But even missing one role can cause the entire process to fall short of the mark or sometimes to start unraveling at the seams.

Consider that if the builder fails to build the right process then in all likelihood other people involved in the process will be unable to perform their jobs effectively. If the design is inappropriate to the desired outcome, the outcome won't be realized. If the process is not designed with process participants in mind, then it will be unwieldy to use creating internal resistance and propagating workarounds.

If process participants do not have an intuitive interface they are unlikely to be effective in using the BPM system. If they do not have obvious and meaningful ways to deal with variances and exceptions, they are likely to push work off to others, avoid addressing problems, or find shortcuts that compromise process goals. Issues will get *covered up*, threatening process transparency.

Without visibility, managers cannot make informed decisions and leadership is perceived by others who work in the process as off the mark. If the process approach does not aggregate and present the information managers need, oversight will have blind spots, direction will be lost and leadership will falter.

The Process is the Sum of the Perspectives

As we've discussed, any given process is really the sum of the perspectives of the people who work on, or in, the process along with their relationships to each other. These perspectives are tightly interwoven, and are critical to successful process work. Effectiveness in anything less than all three process perspectives will dramatically reduce performance, quality and value creation. The failure of organizations to embrace all of three perspectives in process work is what has lead to inconsistency in results from process initiatives.

Considering that processes are nothing more, or less, than the sum of the people who participate in them, it becomes clear what must be done to realize the full potential of business process management. By addressing the sum of all three perspectives holistically the full potential of BPM can be realized in a consistent, predictable and broad-reaching manner.

Two More Perspectives

What we have presented so far reflects traditional process thinking but fails to address two other essential perspectives. This is where strategy and the customer experience are brought into the mix, where we move into the realms of business transformation and creating customer value and loyalty.

Drawing again from the survey by Nathaniel Palmer, we can see from the following chart that transformation is indeed an important part of the process landscape.

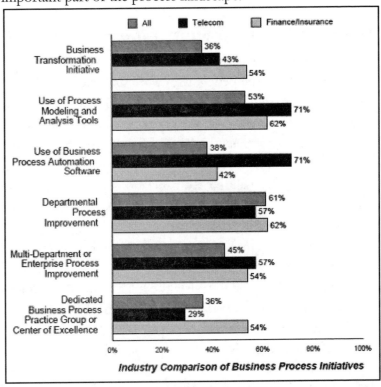

From research by Nathaniel Palmer

Strategy is important and unique enough for us to add another affinity group, *strategists*. Strategists are people who lead transformational process initiatives. They could hold the title of

BPM strategist, director, consultant, champion, specialist or even CEO. Their focus is to achieve business transformation. Transformational process design involves major change to the process at a business model level. However, unlike BPR of days gone by, today strategists take into account the people aspect of process innovation and build in change versus casting processes in concrete.

Strategists will challenge existing assumptions seeking to identify opportunities for process innovation that will dramatically cut costs, improve customer value or enable the organization to adopt a new business model or enter new markets.

By adding the affinity group of strategists to the perspectives model we have almost captured the key perspectives on process. What's still missing?

We started this section by noting that the perspectives of builders, participants and managers are based in large part on the internal perspective of process. Strategists must take into account external perspectives along with the internal perspectives. Yet what affinity group really represents that external perspective of our processes? How about our customers? Do they ever participate in business processes or their design? They certainly can, and quite often do. Customers interact with at least some of our business processes, or else they wouldn't be our customers, would they?

Because customers can participate directly in business processes they can be included in the participants group in the *affinity groups diagram*. But there is another aspect of customers that doesn't fit our normal perspectives on process, the perspective of the customer experience. The customer experience is affected by all of the other perspectives on process. Strategists can design the customer experience into process, builders can develop for it, participants can deliver it and managers can oversee that delivery. So for our diagram, the customer experience moves into the center of the picture, as the customer experience is really what we are doing all of this process stuff for anyway!

From another angle, we can observe that the customer experience is itself a process that is defined by our customers. For example, if a customer is making a purchase then wherever the customer thinks the process starts and ends is indeed where the process starts and ends. Customers don't want to just buy a product or service; they want continuing support over the consumption life cycle of that product or service. The customer process includes the full set of interactions they have with the business and the process must meet the expectations they have with respect to time, effort and money. The customer experiences we create will determine our ultimate success.

Updating the affinity groups diagram to include customers, the customer experience and the strategist group yields a final affinity group diagram as presented below:

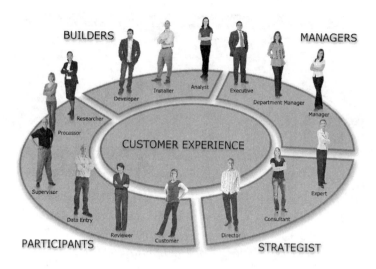

Expanded Affinity Groups Diagram

The customer experience has now become the center of the diagram, the bulls-eye for our process work. It is certainly time for us to realize and accept that everything we do should be done for our customers. Without them, well, we wouldn't exist would we? Updating the common software infrastructure diagram we add strategist as an affinity group and the customer experience as a new layer into the diagram. The use of customer experience as a new layer on top of the diagram visually communicates the point — everything we do, we do for our customers.

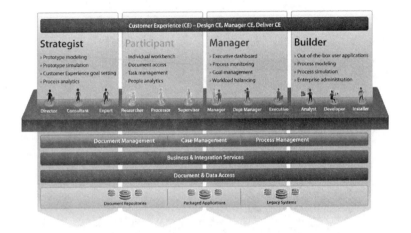

Expanded Common Software Infrastructure for Process

This expanded version of the software infrastructure gives us a more complete perspective on process. The most important takeaway is how the software infrastructure provides the foundation of all the perspectives on process, while perspectives on process become the foundation of the customer experience. This further helps us understand how what we do (including our use of technology) impacts our customers.

Why do we include design, manage and deliver in the customer experience layer? The infrastructure diagram shows us that all affinity groups plus the underpinning software stack are supporting the customer experience. Yet where is the glue? What is shaping, managing and ensuring we deliver the customer experience? As it happens, customer experience is generally an unmanaged result of our processes. Only by designing, managing and delivering customer experiences can our process mastery rise to highest level.

As we work through the seven steps to mastering our processes you will find that we address each of the perspectives we have defined in this chapter. We will address each of the opportunities already discussed or hinted at and tear down each of barriers that stand in our way of process mastery. We start now with step one, understand and embrace your goal.

Step One: Understand and Embrace your Goal

Give me a stock clerk with a goal and I'll give you a man who will make history. Give me a man with no goals and I'll give you a stock clerk. —J.C. Penny

The first step in mastering your business processes is to understand and embrace your business goals. Do you have a goal you are seeking to achieve? Of course you do, otherwise why would you even bother?

Goals define our purpose, and the type of goal we have helps us focus on the kind of improvement actions we must take, along with establishing metrics to determine our degree of success. The one perspective on process that we didn't specifically call out is *you*, and understanding your goal is definitely part of your personal perspective on process. Goals are critical to process participants in the strategist group and they drive the activities of process participants in the builder group.

So what is your goal?

Oh, and if you don't think you have a goal, but instead have a mandate, think again. A mandate or other motivation that requires you to do something with process still means you have a goal because you are expected to do something, something that produces a significant result. For example, your goal may be to meet your organization's expectations of you so you can keep your job and perhaps even qualify for a promotion. If you don't have a specific goal, is it safe for us to say that your goal includes making *something* about the process better? We should certainly hope so.

There are three ways to set process goals that we will cover in this chapter. We will start with financial goals, as they are a common goal shared by almost all organizations.

Financial Goals

Where your goals are financial (cost reduction, increased profit or increased revenue) BPM should be driven by a before-and-after Return on Investment (ROI) analysis. In light of that, here is another interesting process observation from the study by Nathaniel Palmer.

In this study, over one-third of survey respondents did not use ROI analysis as part of their BPM deployments. Further, less than one-sixth of respondents performed any ROI analysis after piloting the project, final roll-out, or as an ongoing assessment. That means that one out of every six BPM projects doesn't have any proof of what the project actually achieved financially nor has any evidence that gains achieved continued to return the initial degree of benefit over time.

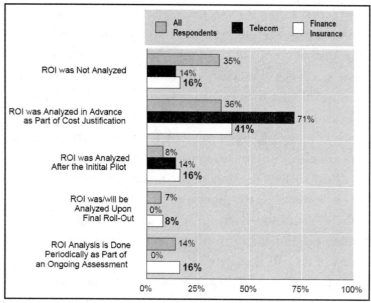

From research by Nathaniel Palmer

Regardless of the reason for this, conducting an ROI analysis of a proposed BPM improvement project is one of the ways we have to set goals for the project. Developing the ROI case and then identifying the measures by which we can assess our success in achieving that ROI is an essential part of process goal setting. It's like taking a vacation where we identify our desired destination, plan our route, determine intermediary stops, create a budget and then head off. Can you imagine taking a vacation where you simply got into the car and randomly drive off whichever way happens to catch your fancy? No directions, no planned stops, and a destination that is somewhere a lot nicer than here? Does that sound like the kind of vacation you want to take? Oh, and what do you think the likely outcome of that approach to vacationing would be? Granted, you might get lucky, but chances are you won't and even poor planning is better than no planning at all.

Yet it seems at times that no planning at all is our approach to process success. But that's not the way to achieve process success, at least not on any consistent or predictable basis.

Is ROI analysis the only way to set process goals? Sure there are. For example, if the process or processes in a particular part of the organization have already been identified as underperforming and in need of overhaul, then we may not deem it necessary to do a ROI analysis.

On a larger scale, ROI becomes a part of the Balanced Scorecard (BSC), a strategic performance management tool for measuring whether the smaller-scale operational activities of a company are aligned with its larger-scale objectives in terms of vision and strategy. By focusing not only on financial outcomes but also on the operational, marketing and developmental inputs to these, the Balanced Scorecard helps provide a more comprehensive view of a business, which in turn helps organizations act in their best long-term interests. Organizations are encouraged to measure, in addition to financial outputs, those factors that influence the financial outputs. For example, process performance, market penetration, long-term learning and skills development, and so on.

The underlying rationale is that organizations cannot directly influence financial outcomes, as these are "lag" measures, and that the use of financial measures alone to inform the strategic control of the firm is unwise.

Organizations should instead also measure those areas where direct management intervention is possible. In so doing, the early versions of the Balanced Scorecard helped organizations achieve a degree of "balance" in selection of performance measures. In practice, early Scorecards achieved this balance by encouraging managers to select measures from three additional categories or perspectives: Customer, Internal Business Processes and Learning and Growth.

It is not sufficient to say we know a process needs improvement. We still need goals for the simple fact that goals (like those derived from an ROI analysis or Balanced Scorecard) force us to assess where we are (the current or as-is state) and where we are going (the to-be state). In effect, goal setting forces us to assess the potential improvement against measures that matter.

Revlon – BPM that Drives EBITDA

Revlon, which takes its name from founders Charles and Joseph Revson along with the chemist on their founding team, Charles Lachman (where the L came from), was founded in 1932. An internationally recognized brand in cosmetics, skin care, fragrances and personal care products, Revlon clocked in 2008 with $1.3 billion in revenues and a healthy 18.4% EBIT-

DA. Not bad. They must be doing something right.

Increasing EBITDA with BPM

Part of what Revlon is doing right is BPM. For example, Revlon has an extremely high claims volume (over 1,000 per day). Before applying BPM (with BPM software) to their claims process, Revlon struggled to keep up with the workload and financial impact was significant with chargebacks amounting to fully 20% of gross revenues. Claims processors were overburdened and were often unable to review low-dollar clams or contest them if appropriate. Another interesting data point was that the document collection process by itself took 30 minutes on average per claim.

In implementing BPM, Revlon reduced processing time by two-thirds (66%) which gave the company the opportunity to process all claims at a net reduction of employee time of over 50%. Revlon has not disclosed the reduction in chargebacks achieved from their use of BPM but with an optimized and streamlined process in place there is little doubt that total chargeback costs would also be reduced (probably quite significantly). Revlon claimed 18-month breakeven and 24 month payback on the project, but what is even more important is the company will reap the cost reduction benefits year after year for many years to come.

Direct cost reduction, as a non-discounted or amortized savings. In the Revlon case it is estimated to be in the range of $1.2 - $1.5 million per year without factoring in other benefits derived from the BPM improvement. That translates to a minimum half point gain in EBITDA. Now *that* is the way to leverage BPM. Revlon reduced processing time by 66% and realized a net reduction of 50% in labor time.

Is reduction in processing time a valid process goal? Sure it is. We can measure and contrast it with before and after measurements. Reduction in processing time is a different take on financially driven ROI because reduction in process time will reduce the operating costs of the process.

This example is important as it shows a use of BPM where reduced operating costs through process improvement made the company more efficient while lowering its operating cost, resulting in a direct impact on the bottom line of the business.

So what did Revlon do that made this BPM initiative successful? Well for one thing the company knew its baseline, its challenges and it measured the result of their efforts. While we may not know what Revlon expected to achieve, the company certainly achieved success and undoubtedly improved its ability to leverage BPM for future successes by conducting the before and after analysis.

Now some of us will shy from doing a ROI or Balance Scorecard measurement analysis, especially one that includes before and after measurement, particularly when we aren't expected to do so. Measurements can be problematic as they will either validate or invalidate our expected results. While validating our results is fine, invalidating them is not comfortable for many people.

Yet how else will we know, really know, what we achieved? Whether the results are on target, above or below target, knowing the results tells us something. It can validate our assumptions, help us adjust our expectations, teach us to capitalize on what really works, and help us improve on what didn't work as expected.

KPIs for Goals

In addition to financial ROI or Balanced Scorecard measures, we have other ways to establish baselines, set goals and measure our success. One of those ways is to use Key Performance Indicators (KPIs).

KPIs accurately reflect what we want to improve about the process. KPIs could come from a mandate, a compliance requirement, a service initiative or even a specific process outcome that we can clearly see is undesirable.

Mandates could be improvements in measures such as error reduction, meeting government regulations, business partner requirements, defect reduction, response time improvement, and so on. These motivations for improvement often arise from a sense of dissatisfaction—an *undesirable outcome.*

As in the case of ROI analysis, identifying the metrics that describe the nature of the undesirable outcome gives us a baseline for comparison. From that baseline we can define the KPIs we need for goal setting and the metrics to assess the degree of success we expect to achieve from our process improvement efforts. In this case we are defining the current or as-is process state by its underperforming metrics and we will be describing our goals by improvement targets against that same set of metrics. Like financial goals, this gives us the means to:

- Be rigorous in our assessment of what we can achieve
- Establish a clear deliverable that we can hold ourselves accountable against
- Measure our success against our expected results

The undesirable outcome can also be related to enterprise or stakeholder dissatisfaction. We often see this reflected in profit or revenue strategies, where executive leadership is concerned or focused in elevating value. Again, using KPIs gives organizations the means to assess where they are, where they are going, and then to judge how well they deliver on their goals.

KPI Variant – Customer KPIs for Goals

The third way to set goals is a variant on the KPI approach for goal setting. It comes from focusing on customers by acknowledging that the customer experience organizations currently provide may be lacking in what they could or should deliver to their customers. For companies that are seeking to excel in service value or for whom customer loyalty is of high value, this approach is vital.

In this scenario we identify customer KPIs for starters. Customer KPIs represent what customers care about and are an external perspective of an organization's processes (commonly termed an outside-in perspective).

As with the discussion on KPIs in general, we must identify what customer KPIs are in order to create a baseline. From there it becomes a matter of establishing goals against customer KPIs, followed by assessing success after process improvement is implemented. Once more we have the means to be rigorous in our assessment of what can be achieved, and we can establish a clear deliverable that we can hold ourselves accountable to and measure our success against.

Any of these methods, financial ROI, Balanced Scorecard, KPIs or Customer-specific KPIs, enable us to develop an understanding of where we are, where we want to go, and to know when we get there. Assuming we have our goals in place the next step is to process mastery is to build the exceptional processes that will deliver on those goals.

Step Two:
Build an Elegant Design

Simplicity is the ultimate sophistication. —Leonardo Da Vinci

If process builders (designers, analysts, developers, etc.) hope to produce exceptional results then they must create exceptional process designs, what may be termed as *elegant* process design. Building an elegant design requires having a process model, observing it critically and then simplifying it in order to achieve improvement. This applies even when we are seeking conformance or compliance because the *simplest good design* is far more likely to produce the desired process outcome than is the *best complex design*.

While that fact seems to still elude many people, it's glaringly obvious that the big winners in BPM all share one thing in common – they all build simplified versions of the process in their improvement activity. It really doesn't matter what the goal is, if we really seek to improve a process then simplification is our holy grail.

Of course that also means smart simplification. To paraphrase Albert Einstein, "Everything should be made as simple as possible, but no simpler." If a process is only capable of marginally supporting its intended purpose or outcome then simplification could make it even less capable of doing so. Further, some complexity is brought into business processes with the use of technology, which is itself a form of complexity. Yet at the end of the day, it is the well-designed process that simplifies what people do and relegates automation by software to simple, service-based concepts that hit the home-runs.

Simplicity is the Ultimate Sophistication

Five centuries years ago, Leonardo da Vinci drew the conclusion that *simplicity is the ultimate sophistication* from his practice of observation and description. His approach blended both art and science and is seen as the forerunner of modern systems theory and complexity schools of thought. His statement is the foundation of good, even great, processes.

Process masters shed complexity by rigorously challenging process design work from a mindset based on one simple question: "Is there any way to make this even simpler?" Sounds simple, but no matter how simple we think it sounds, challenging our own assumptions is never easy.

Assumptions are deeply embedded habits or thinking patterns that operate within us on autopilot. But to really master process, we can't let our minds run on autopilot. We need to bite the bullet and take ourselves into a state of cognitive awareness if we expect to uncover the most powerful opportunities for improving our processes. Just remember, it's *your mindset* and you can do want you want to with it.

Let's test your abilities to move outside of your assumptions. Given the following maze, take a few minutes right now to find the path from start to finish that has the least number of turns.

Start

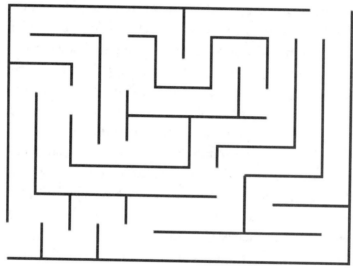

Finish

Find the path from Start to Finish with the least turns.
Do not proceed until you complete this exercise.

What did you find? Did your path take less than 20 turns? Less than 15? Less than 10?

Remember your answer, we will return to the maze exercise in a moment to explore the purpose of the exercise in further detail.

So the process builder's mindset is the key to unlocking simplicity. If we aren't willing to challenge our own assumptions to make things simpler, we are not going to make it simpler for other process participants. Instead, when asked if the process is being simplified we are likely to be told something along the lines of "the process is much simpler, we've encoded all of the complexity into the model so the software can handle it." If you hear an answer like that, or any variation that sounds at all similar, you can rest assured that the process is already rigid and brittle before the first piece of work goes through it. Why? In this case assumptions have *not* been challenged, and complexity has just been moved from one place to another.

Because of the need for simplification, one of the process builder's essential tools of the trade is the capability of process automation within BPM software. When coupled with an overall emphasis on generalized process simplification this becomes a powerful mechanism to reduce costs, improve efficiency and reduce errors. Process automation is both an improvement mechanism as well as a simplification mechanism (or at least it can be when used correctly). This is precisely where cognitive science enters the picture with respect to process modeling and process improvement.

Now back to our maze exercise. We asked before if your path from start to finish too less than 10 turns. Now we ask, did your path take less than five turns?

If it did, then your path from start to finish probably looks something like this:

Start

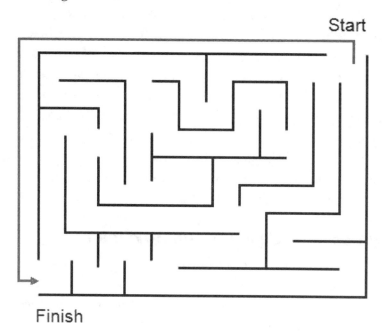

Finish

This path from start to finish only takes three turns, right? But wait a minute! Isn't that cheating?

The point is not to cheat, but to cognitively review what just happened. No rules were given that required you to follow the rules of a maze that you probably applied to the problem automatically. You may not have done so, but when given an exercise like this most people will apply the rules they already know without thinking. That is the point – most people automatically apply or conform to the rules of what they already know.

Applied to process this concept takes on an interesting aspect. Where processes are already documented, or where we document process by creating a detailed model of the *as is process model*, we create assumptions that are far too often left unchallenged. Put in other words, *the existing shape of the process imposes constraints on what we perceive as opportunities to dramatically improve the process.* Yet all processes exist to serve a purpose (they better!) and our challenge in simplifying process is to find the simplest and most elegant way to produce that outcome – the shortest path from start to finish.

Process Modeling for Improvement

In working with process modeling as part of process improvement, one of the first challenges is the lack of existing process documentation—or the *over abundance of it.* Either condition can make it very challenging to even get started.

So what do we do if we don't have any process documentation, particularly no process model representing the existing process design? Or for that matter, what if we have the existing process model and when printed it would fill an entire wall or more? Are there ways to handle these scenarios?

The answer is yes on both accounts. When seeking to improve processes [1] it's important to note that if we don't have them already documented, this is not a difficult challenge for us to address. As long as we know what we want to improve, what the undesirable outcome is, we can track down the activities that produce it by documenting the process behind the outcome. Documenting the process behind the outcome is a simple way to create a high-level overview of what is happening in a given process.

This should be a fairly simple exercise, even when dealing with very complex processes. At most, complex processes *may* require more time but only within a very reasonable context because we are dealing with a high-level process view.

But why the high-level process view? The high-level process view gives us a unique perspective, one that has few distractions to vie for our attention. In this case the old saying that "the devil is in the details" is certainly true. Details definitely vie for our attention, forcing us to focus on much smaller segments of a process, one at a time. Obviously, we aren't going to get the *big picture* when that happens, and the *big picture* is exactly what we need to be working with.

For perspective, it may help to relate the process to an activity in which you have already participated. Many organiza-

---

[1] Process improvement, in this context, refers to significant improvement based on a new project, not on incremental improvement based on the statistical analysis that some BPM products are capable of performing for processes already modeled.

tions run workshops that include documenting high-level process models. The resources used in these workshops are often nothing more than brown paper and post-it notes. If you haven't participated in a workshop like that, or even if you have, it's worth our time to review a common workshop format.

The workshop exercise starts by taping or tacking a piece of brown paper on a wall, usually at least four times as wide as it is high. That creates the overall process canvas. Next, post-it notes representing steps (or activities or tasks) are used to write down a descriptive name for each step of the process. This is usually done with a team (3 to 4 is statistically the best number of people on the team) with very few rules to the exercise, allowing the team to find a style with which it is comfortable.

Once all of the steps have been identified and written down they are then stuck onto the brown paper in the order they occur in the process. Sometimes teams stick the post-its on the brown paper as they go, other times they identify all of the steps and then put the post-its on the brown paper.

How many steps should you have? Most likely you will have somewhere between eight and fifty. Less than eight suggests that you may have gone to *high* or have focused on a process fragment, not an overall process. Over fifty suggests that you may be making the exercise more complicated than it needs to be, which can be a slippery slope into the highly undesirable state of complexity. The high-level process model is nothing more, or less, than the process skeleton of steps or activities in the process. Sometimes we think of these as the major steps or activities, to help us avoid too much detail. At this level even the most complicated processes are relatively simple to model.

The next thing we do is create the new, or *to be*, shape of the process. In this exercise we challenge the process, making sure to recognize that identifying actions that can be taken to produce an elegant process design requires a mix of cognitive science and perhaps a little art. More than anything else, high-level modeling provides a way for people to focus their awareness, concentration and observational skills onto the process in a way that enables them to challenge the process assumptions as well as their own.

For instance, it should be obvious that removing, combining, automating or simplifying process activities will usually make a process more efficient. Yet judging the potential value (versus effort required to implement the improvement) is sometimes an art, not a science. We must apply common sense and the experience we have accumulated in our professional lives to answer questions of this nature. Not all simplifications have the same value or the same cost. Such perspectives need to be surfaced by the team. Yet there are some principles we can apply that will help us in crafting the desired process shape. These principles include:

1. Challenge artifacts, ensuring that they are "value-add."
2. Identify and eliminate hand-offs where possible.

Eliminate what is Not Relevant to the Goal

It's no news that change is the only constant, but processes tend to act like out-of-date garbage collectors. Business rules, activities, organizational structure, volume assumptions, and so on all build up within processes – and stay there until we remove them.

Gertie the Dinosaur,
Winsor McKay
1914

Is your process a
Dinosaur?

If we aren't careful, our processes soon begin to take on the form of dinosaurs. Business rules and activities become so far out of date that the reason they are there doesn't exist anymore. But if we don't take the garbage out, then of course it stays right where we put it.

We can only ferret out this garbage by challenging the process's steps, activities, tasks and rules to ensure that each one is making a value-added contribution to our desired outcome. This is how to identify improvements, how to reshape a process to meet current needs and maximize process success. Once we know non value-added process elements are there, we can then take actions to eliminate them.

It is, in fact, necessary for us to challenge each step and activity in the process to ensure that it is in fact necessary, that it adds value by its contribution to the desired outcomes. If it doesn't add value it shouldn't be there. In many cases our processes include characteristics that are no longer relevant to our needs as they exist today.

Just because process builders don't know these out-of-date process artifacts are there doesn't mean that that they don't exist. Process participants who actually do the work in our processes already know about these artifacts because they have to live with them. Their lives are complicated and their job satisfaction reduced because they have to live with process garbage every single day. Removing all non value-add actions is essential to maximizing success and has the added benefit of improving employee morale and job satisfaction.

Hand-offs, White-space and Break Points

The late Dr. William Edwards Deming is noted for his work

on quality starting in the 1940s. In many ways, Deming is the person who drove the management and improvement thinking that lead to the creation of Six Sigma. Dr. Deming was instrumental in making the observation that manufacturing quality control, when held to tolerances better than required by specifications, produced products that worked smoother, longer and served their design purpose better than those that were just in tolerance. From this was borne the original concept and theory behind Six Sigma.

Dr. William Edwards Deming

Deming's other major contribution to management philosophy was the idea of *white space* which he characterized as the "interface points, or the handoff points, where most of the action and the screw-ups occur." Deming clearly articulated, and was primarily concerned with, hand-offs between functional areas of the organization, recognizing that these hand-offs were one of the most prominent sources of inefficiency, non valued-added work, and internal conflict within organizations.

Further, Deming's work placed both his observations on quality per Six Sigma and white-space handoffs within the larger context of process. It is clear that Deming recognized that organizations are effectively the "sum of their processes" and his management philosophies have this theme woven throughout them. Deming was adamant about the importance of understanding processes from the perspective of customers, producers, and suppliers. While this theme is essential to understanding process work, Deming's overall philosophy remains a gaping hole in the management approach of many organizations. What is the takeaway?

Look for hand-offs in the white space, and eliminate as much of it as you can. Hand-offs are a source of non-value added work that should be eliminated where ever possible, and where elimination is not possible then they should at least be streamlined. Sounds simple, doesn't it? Unfortunately it is not as simple as it sounds.

Much of the existing structure in our organizations that forms the basis for how we do work stems from our internal and departmental perspectives (silos). This internal perspective is difficult for us to observe and challenges us because of the nature of how we think of what we do in our jobs.

Jeff Hawkins' book, *On Intelligence,* is recommended for helping us better understand how our intelligence works.

On Intelligence by Jeff Hawkins

In the book, we are presented with a theory for intelligent machine design, or at least that is the stated purpose of the book. The book offers an entirely different value proposition that provides the context behind why it can be so difficult to challenge the processes we work within on a daily basis.

On Intelligence is in many ways an exploratory journey into why we do what we do. The book helps us to develop a much deeper understanding of our cognitive interactions with the world around us.

Perhaps the most important takeaways from this book are the six cognitive levels of our minds, and how at the lowest level we operate virtually on auto-pilot while at the highest level we are fully engaged in cognitive awareness. That's a lot more important than most of us realize because it is only when we are at the higher cognitive levels that we can gain those insights that make such a big difference. At the lower cognitive levels we are stuck in repetitive, even rote, behavior that may produce some value but falls far short of our potential. Insight, innovation, market value, and the big wins all stem from observations processed at higher levels of cognition. *On Intelligence* is a great reference for increasing our understanding of this phenomenon we call the human mind.

Using the intelligence theory presented in the book, we all have six levels of cognitive awareness. The level with which we process sensory input is primarily driven by the uniqueness of the input we are receiving. Put in laymen's terms, when you see (smell, feel or hear) something that doesn't fit with what you already know then you process that information at a higher cognitive level. For instance, when you drive somewhere, do you observe each vehicle around you such that you can talk about it, how it was shaped, what color it was, and so forth? Certainly not. What if you see a roadster as if it came right out of the movie American Graffiti?

Original Milner's Coupe from American Graffiti

Seeing this car is highly likely to draw your attention, elevating our level of cognitive awareness. We are far more likely to remember this car, and numerous details about it, than we are the other vehicles on the road around us. Yet those vehicles are there, are they not? Of course they are, but they are relegated to a lower level of cognition that in many cases is so low that we don't even notice that our minds have processed the input.

So when we seek to challenge a process with respect to hand offs or white spaces, we need to push ourselves to challenge the assumptions around us. Just because we currently perform work in a certain way does not mean it is the right way to work. We must challenge our assumptions and dig into the reasons why things are the way they are.

Doing nothing more than repeatedly asking *why* will peel off assumptions, layer after layer, until we get to the root cause of why we do what we do. Finding that root cause of *why* we do things a particular way is the key to uncovering opportunities for process improvement that would otherwise be missed.

Acerta:
Reducing Costs while Enhancing Service

Uncovering opportunities can often bring multiple value streams into the process improvement plan. For example, if you could decrease costs while enhancing customer service with one improvement action that would certainly be of high value to the organization, wouldn't it?

That is exactly what Acerta did with BPM. Acerta, a leading human resource service provider in Belgium with over 1,200 employees and revenue in excess of 135 million Euros, was challenged with paper storage limitations. The company was running out of storage capacity. Yet the cost of increasing physical storage couldn't be financially justified. Acerta needed to move to electronic document storage and in doing so they saw the opportunity to also improve their business processes and enhance customer services.

Acerta employed a BPM system with document handling facilities to reduce storage requirements. But they also used the BPM system to automate operations and improve the ability of their staff to access customer information in near real time as well as to provide multi-user access to documents.

Having already delved deeply into the challenges faced by

the front-line customer service representatives (CSRs), Acerta deployed the BPM system to solve the storage problem with a process design that would empower their CSRs to offer a higher level of customer service in less time at lower cost.

Further, Acerta piloted the new system with a target group of CSRs to ensure the new system would meet their needs before rolling it out for the entire company. The pilot group validated the benefits of the process design in the BPM system. With that validation in hand, the process was rolled out to the rest of the organization resulting in a marked increase in customer satisfaction and productivity, coupled with a reduction in operating costs (both storage and labor). The project was a resounding success on all fronts.

Acerta – Reducing Costs while Enhancing Customer Service

Let's turn our attention to the process *backbone*, the executable process design and the points of inflection between the technology being used and the people who must interact with that technology once it is deployed. Though it is certainly much easier for process builders to concentrate on the executable model, doing so will leave much potential off the table and can even lead to process disaster. After all, the critical differentiator in the use of BPM technology is its ability to serve the needs of the people who actually do the work in a process.

Thus while the executable process design is essential, the most valuable output from process design is the high-level process model, the shape of the process that is aligned to the people who actually do the work in a process. Fortunately, high-level processing modeling does indeed appear to be one of the most common practices in BPM today even though much work has been devoted to more detailed and complicated forms of process modeling needed for sophisticated processes and their choreographed execution.

For example, the Business Process Modeling Notation (BPMN) is a process modeling standard from the Object Management Group (OMG). The latest revision, BPMN 2.0, goes into significant detail on the finer points of process modeling in its 500 pages, but it seems that actual use of BPMN involves a very small subset of the full specification.

One of the most relevant studies regarding BPMN usage comes from Dr. Jan Recker and Dr. Michael zur Muehlen.

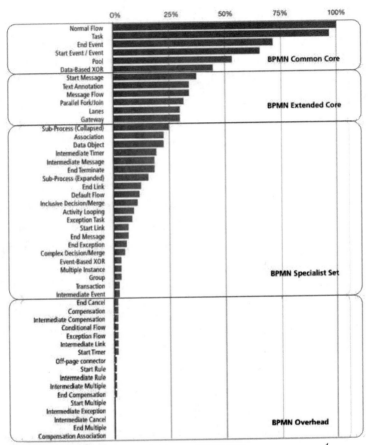

Frequency distributions of BPMN construct usage[1]

---

[1] zur Muehlen, M., Recker, J. (2008): How Much Language is Enough? Theoretical and Practical Use of the Business Process Modeling Notation. In Z. Bellahsene and M. Leonard (eds.): Advanced Information Systems Engineering - CAiSE 2008. Lecture Notes in Computer Science, Vol. 5074. Springer, Montpellier, France, pp. 465-479. Copyright Springer-Verlag.

From research based on actual use by end-user organizations, the study uncovered frequency of use for BPMN as shown in the distribution diagram above. The report from the study, entitled *How Much Language is Enough? Theoretical and Practical Use of the Business Process Modeling Notation* indicates that only two of the fifty BPMN constructs covered are used by almost every person modeling a process. Those two constructs, *Normal Flow and Tasks*, are the essence of high-level process modeling.

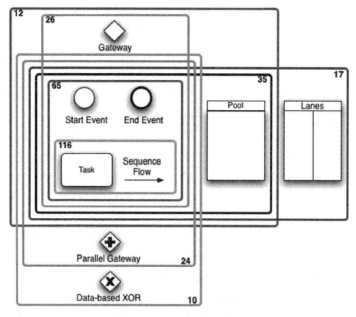

Grouping of BPMN Elements

This reality is reinforced even further in the same report

with a graph that demonstrates how constructs are used *together*.

This might also explain the popularity of the book, *The Process: Business Process Modeling Using BPMN*, by Alexander Grosskopf, Gero Decker, and Mathias Weske). [1] While other books go into great detail about the notation, the notation isn't the issue; just go to OMG's BPMI.org and download the specifications. The critical issue is instilling a way of thinking that brings shared insight into the process of process modeling; something more a matter of thought patterns than notation. *The Process* uses a fast-paced novel format that is based on a real company that the authors guided through the process modeling process. This book is about process thinking, and process modeling as the path to business innovation.

Research clearly indicates that the common industry practice is that of high-level process modeling. The implications are important, suggesting that the process builders are indeed working with high-level *as is* process models and *to be* process designs. With either version of the high-level process model process builders have a useful basis for creating an elegant process design.

But what do we do if we don't have that process model to start with? What if we don't even have any goals identified when we begin the challenge of crafting an executable process model? We want the backbone to be what helps us realize the goals we have set, but if we have no clearly defined and action-

---

[1] www.bpmnbook.com

able goals then how can we deliver on them?

The reality is that most of the time goals either don't exist or have not been properly articulated. This leaves us in the unenviable position of building the process backbone without clarity on what we are expected to build. So when goals do not exist on a process project, it's back to Step One.

Simplification through Automation

Much has been said about the benefits of automating business processes to the greatest extent possible. While the general concept of automation is certainly attractive, and indeed is often beneficial, automation only adds value when it is used for the right reasons.

Automation should be used for steps, activities, and tasks that don't require human oversight or involvement. The best designed processes keep people focused on doing the things only people can do.

BPM technology capabilities are often a key factor in successfully automating business processes. Perhaps the most important automation opportunity is the elimination of paper documents from business processes. Paper documents are a process artifact that is largely irrelevant to what we do today, and how we do it. Yet very few organizations have successfully gone paperless, particularly with the business processes that involve the core products of the business.

We are still processing paper-driven activities in the vast majority of organizations. Only for completely online transactions do we see this area of operations automated with any frequency. In many business processes, people are filling out paper forms then other people are entering the data from these paper forms into a computer system. Yet another group of people are reviewing the data against the physical document, and all along the way these pieces of paper are being handled by more and more people to get them from one group to the next. Does that sound like an efficient process to you?

As we can easily imagine, somehow when handling paper some of that paper manages to get in the wrong place. It gets lost in the shuffle, and when it does the people in our organizations must find it no matter where it may have ended up. So there are also people who file, store, retrieve and track down the paper in our processes.

The next place where automation is likely to create significant benefit is in the automation of multiple system interactions. The systems we use in our organizations to get work done are often point solutions with significant isolation. They were implemented to solve a particular problem but rarely play well with the other applications we use. The result is a number of siloed applications that don't play well with one another.

Those who do the work in our organizations end up moving in and out of multiple software applications to get work done. Needless to say, this situation is inefficient and highly prone to producing errors. Using automation to reduce multiple system interactions down to single interactions, or even a fully-automated transaction, can have a major impact on process effectiveness.

Expecting employees to move in and out of multiple systems, often requiring them to enter the same information in multiple software systems, is just plain bad process design. Automation that triggers multiple system interactions behind one human process interaction (where multiple human interactions were required before) reduces processing time and errors, while simplifying job training and knowledge requirements.

As stated earlier, if a task doesn't need to be done by people then we should automate it if possible. Digitized documents, systems interactions and multiple systems interactions are automation opportunities that can be leveraged when improving business processes.

Another automation concept of importance is that of process orchestration. The concept of process orchestration can best be described as how work flows through a process. BPM systems embed initial orchestration from the design of the process model. For example, work is moved through the process under a programmatic workflow model that often includes rules to address specific work types, volumes, and resource scenarios.

The value derived from this kind of process orchestration varies from significant to very little. Where existing processes are poorly orchestrated, characterized by repeated instances of chaotic activity as people try to sort out next steps in their work, the value is high. Where process organization is dealing with operating scenarios already smoothly running, introducing programmatic orchestration is likely to add limited value and may even be detrimental to operations based on the rigidity of the programmatic orchestration model.

This occurs because process models are defined by rules based on knowledge at hand. In many cases where operations appear to be running smoothly, you can bet that there are many adaptations and workarounds that never make it into the process model.

And complex rule set matrices don't help either. Complex models for process automation become rigid very quickly, and automated processes are much harder to adapt to continual changes than even their non-automated cousins. While we may not know the exact point where a process moves into an exception state, we do know that it happens, and once it does, change becomes a project effort that requires experts with deep knowledge of each process that needs to be modified. The rule of thumb is that the more complex the process, the more rigid, costly and less agile the process becomes.

One way to mitigate some of this complexity is to break processes into logical, independent chunks by using sub-processes and services (as in SOA, Service-Oriented Architecture). Just remember that creating or using sub-processes or SOA services is not the full solution. The solution is to break processes into independent components that can be changed when they are the source of misalignment to the current state. This actually begins happening the moment a new process model is created because all process models are effectively a snapshot of what we knew at a given moment in time. Breaking a process into independent components is very similar to the concept used in the *Agile* method of software development – a concept that is just as applicable to process design as it is software development.

A more adaptive use of automation in BPM comes from the capability to manually orchestrate part of a process. In this scenario, managers and supervisors are given the interface they need to adjust work rules on demand, with automation behind that interface able to provision service-oriented process adaptations on the fly. The result is that changes are provisioned without needing help from process experts or IT professionals. This is adaptive process orchestration, and we will discuss this subject further in the chapter, *Orchestrating Resources to Real-Time Demand.*

In summary, automation of steps, activities, and tasks is the first place we should look for improving our business processes while process orchestration is the next. But automation opportunities also exist within steps, activities, and tasks that we cannot completely automate.

Simplifying Tasks through Automation

Simplifying tasks through automation requires us to deal with validation, contextual relevance, data entry reduction and error elimination. We commonly see this type of automation for interfaces like purchase pages and sign-up forms on Web sites. Some of the most common types include:

- Formatted text entry elements: e.g., for phone numbers
- Drop down lists: e.g., for selecting Country or State
- Linked form objects: a given selection introduces an additional linked form element
- Data reuse: e.g., a checkbox to select an address for shipping
- Suggested text matches: e.g., the Google search element
- Creation of passwords with double entry to reduce errors

What we are seeking to accomplish with these forms of automation is always the same. We are simplifying the user experience, and challenging ourselves to identify what we can do that is likely to make it easier for the person interacting with the interface to do so successfully.

One of the least leveraged forms of automation is the concept of single entry. How often we do find interfaces that require the user to enter the same information more than once. Aside from password creation, which uses double entry to confirm we have typed in the password we want, there is no sense in making a person entry the same data twice. It is redundant, a waste of time, and increases the chances of making errors.

In many systems, if an error is made for duplicate data, it can spawn off a number of undesirable consequences. For example, entering the same data twice with an error can cause systems to treat the information as dissociated records, as if they are entirely different entities. Not only can this break data relationships it can also cause multiple ID creation against a single entity. This is the reason why some people receive multiple mailers or notices with only a letter or two different in the address information.

Like Google does with its search entries, we can automatically create a list of likely search queries as a search string is typed. In this way, the desired search query, or a query that is more likely to return the results we want, is often presented to the user as a selectable choice. This reduces the time spent in typing search queries. This approach can even help us to refine what we enter into text fields in an online form.

What else can we do? What about the case where the response to one question, or the information entered in one field, can change what is expected of us? For example, if credit score is part of the requirement for a certain loan program and is a hard rule (less than 650 does not qualify) then wouldn't it make sense to obtain that information first? Especially considering that for applicants that fail to pass this criterion, the process is effectively done? In this case, the *order* in which data is entered has the potential to dramatically simplify the user experience if we back it with automatic qualification.

Yet all too often this kind of automation is missing from process designs. One more thing. How do you think the employees feel that have to enter in all loan application data first before submitting it for processing only to see a certain portion of those applications rejected by the credit check (assuming it runs once the completed application is submitted)? You can bet they aren't happy about that. Put another way, how would you feel if 20% of the application forms you work on are rejected because of a rule that if applied on the front end of the process, would have removed the necessity of doing all that non value-added work?

While many organizations are building this kind of effective automation into their processes there are still more that are not. Reordering tasks and checking those variables that can determine on the spot whether we continue to process the work or not is an important example of task simplification.

The most challenging idea often arising in this area of process design is that modelers don't always know where problems or opportunities exist. But they can learn where some task automation opportunities exist simply by looking at the work of the process task or activity. We can see automation opportunities just by taking some time with the process and challenging how work gets done now. But that usually won't find everything, because the one thing missing from this kind of approach is context.

Context has to do with what really happens when people do work. The best way to really know where opportunities exist in getting work done is to get out there and observe – step into the shoes of the process participant. Asking people who work in the process may surface a few nuggets of gold, and watching what people do, and how they do it, is what will uncover the mother lode of automation opportunities. That is the beginning of the conversation on personal productivity, which starts in the next chapter and is the 3rd step we take in achieving process mastery.

Step Three: Improve Personal Productivity

Being busy does not always mean real work. The object of all work is production or accomplishment and to either of these ends there must be forethought, system, planning, intelligence, and honest purpose, as well as perspiration. Seeming to do is not doing. —Thomas Alva Edison

Personal productivity is the secret sauce that drives some organizations to excel, even in difficult times, while others always seem one step shy of getting their act together. More often than not, personal productivity is a rollercoaster ride of responding to improvements that do positively impact productivity but that are not sustainable. That is, of course, when the rollercoaster comes roaring down from the peak that it ground its way up to with so much effort.

In reviewing business sector productivity over the last 60 years, the data collected and collated by the U.S. Bureau of Labor Statistics paints an interesting picture. What we see from this point of view is that productivity is indeed a cyclical event rather than a gain that keeps forever.

It's highly likely that there are a number of factors behind this cyclical pattern in productivity but it is at least driven in part by bad processes, or perhaps it would be better to say *band-aid* processes.

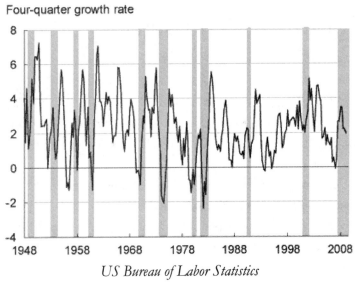

Four-quarter growth rate

US Bureau of Labor Statistics
Business Sector Productivity – Last 60 Years

Band-Aids – Not a Cure for Corporate Ills

A band-aid process starts out as an under-performing process that needs to be improved. Band-aid processes are commonly placed under software control, often have complex process models, frequently embed many business rules in the process software and almost all are built from a command and control perspective. Sounds like a pretty heavy-duty band-aid?

The reason why we call these band-aid processes is that they focus on the symptom rather than the cause. With the band-aid applied, the process is likely to head right back into the poor performance category. There are two influences that guarantee that will happen.

First, there is the matter of context that we began talking about in the previous chapter. *Context* includes all of the environmental, societal, and behavioral influences that affect how work gets done. There is no place that this is more obvious than in the trenches with the people doing the work in our processes. The people who perform the work are exposed to significant contextual influences from both internal and external sources. Internal management and infrastructure changes are biggies, but sometimes even small changes in human resource policies can have a profound effect. Changing shift times, overtime policies and documentation for things like sick-time approval (did you bring your doctor's note, Johnny?) can have negative effects on process performance.

Meanwhile the world outside is changing at a rate like never before, imposing pressure on our processes that, for brittle over-engineered processes, causes them to strain and break. If you want to be a mechanical or aeronautical engineer, then go build bridges or rocket ships, not business processes. Processes that people interact with require a highly subjective engineering exercise that in turn requires a unique blend of cognitive science. In fact no one should be designing processes without having read the works of Donald Norman, a founder of the

Institute for Cognitive Science.

In his book *The Design of Everyday Things*, Norman describes the psychology behind what he deems good and bad design, through case studies, and proposes design principles. He exalts the importance of design in our everyday lives, and the consequences of errors caused by bad design.

The Design of Everyday Things by Donald Norman

In this book, Norman uses the term "user-centered design" to describe design based on the needs of the user, leaving aside what he deems secondary issues like aesthetics. User-centered design involves simplifying the structure of tasks, making things visible, getting the mapping right, exploiting the powers of constraint, designing for error, explaining affordances and seven stages of action.

What should we use to help us place the dividing line between what will enable people to maintain productivity gains versus over-engineered processes that are likely to crack under pressure?

As one example, we can look at the perspective taken by Netflix. Netflix is in the movie business, or perhaps it is better to say they are in the personal movie and TV viewing business. However you prefer to define what they do, Netflix has rapidly become a dominant market player in rental and on-demand consumption of movies and TV shows. With over 10 million customers and revenue on track in 2009 to hit over $1.5 billion (with gross margins of 30+% and rising) the company is delivering on its promise.

What is Netflix's promise to their customers? Netflix promises to deliver customer satisfaction. Customers agree that Netflix delivers on their promise with over 90% of surveyed customers saying that they would recommend Netflix service to a friend. They promise to keep making the best service even better. They promise the best content selection, personalized choices and 24/7 free customer support. They appear to be delivering on their promises quite well and they use process to help in a very interesting way.

The movie and TV show rental business (DVD's or on demand) is a low margin business. There isn't much room for making mistakes and there certainly is no room for premium pricing. That means Netflix is selling a commodity product in a highly competitive market. Do you think process is important in a business like that?

Process is essential to companies like Netflix, so much so that we might jump to the conclusion that highly engineered and refined processes are critical to their success. While this may be true in cases like the actual processing and shipping of physical DVDs, in reality it is the initial innovative design of that process that makes the real difference. That design has most material moving out of distribution centers the same day it moves in, keeping the majority of inventory *afloat* in the U.S. Postal system. The biggest challenge is managing all of the processes that a company with roughly 1,300 employees simply cannot do without.

However, in a presentation by Netflix CEO Reed Hastings uploaded to www.slideshare.com, some very interesting observations on process emerge. Mr. Hastings observes that as most companies grow in size they use process to control their environment, an act that reduces personal freedom. The mindset we commonly find is that by developing highly structured processes we can increase consistency while reducing the number of errors produced.

Mr. Hastings continues in the presentation to describe a phenomenon where growth increases complexity to a degree that injects chaos into the mix when balanced against the behaviors of high performance employees. Highly structured processes are used to drive out chaos by most companies, but in doing so they also drive out high performance employees.

What a minute. That seems to be a bit challenging, doesn't it? It seems that we have a choice. We can either exist in a permanent state of chaos with lots of high performance people or we can operate in a state of unity knowing we will lose most of our top talent. Talk about the lesser of two evils.

Further complicating the situation is the fact that keeping those top talents is an essential ingredient in adapting to rapid market change. Conversely, implementing a highly structured process is a great way to maximize short term financial success.

If we don't put this into perspective our process direction can really jump the track. Remember the productivity graph from the U.S. Bureau of Labor Statistics? The cyclical nature of business productivity is at least partially the result of over-structured processes that quickly lose their relevance to our context as the world around us keeps changing.

One key observation that we can make is that regardless of we want from our processes, our target is constantly on the move. In fact, neither the target nor the process stands still. Because change is a given, then the more complicated, structured and controlled our processes become the more likely they are to inhibit our ability to adapt to changes as they occur. In fact, every process that is designed, optimized, or improved and then deployed is out of date before we even turn it on. How can that be?

It's simple really; we can only improve and implement

changes to processes aimed at a fixed target. Now if our time span is weeks or months there is probably so little movement (change) that we are effectively working on the current context of the process. But for those who still believe in the four year master plan, can you imagine how much change is likely to occur in four years? Just look back at what has changed in the last four years and you'll have a good idea of what we mean.

Command and control processes, which are still very much a part of many companies, go out of date even faster and are much harder to bring back up to date. They are band-aid processes that become less and less aligned to our needs and changing contexts with every passing day. That's why we often see immediate improvements, but when we go back a year or two later and reassess the process we find we aren't in any better shape than we were before the last improvement cycle. The benefits don't stick because we designed the process for a specific context that doesn't exist anymore, and then began applying band-aids.

The lesson to be learned is that tightly aligning a process to the current context, including embedding everything we can up to and sometimes including the kitchen sink in it, is a recipe for productivity disaster. Any gains are short lived, forcing us to continually reengineer the entire process. The approach we must take needs to strike a balance – a balance between people and process.

Balancing People and Process

Improving personal productivity on an ongoing basis requires that we seek an optimal balance between process structure and personal freedom. Simplicity once again enters the discussion here, because simplifying process models and user interactions and experiences reduces complexity – that's precisely where Donald Norman's user-centered design principles come in. Being that complexity is the reason brittle and rigid processes formed in the first place, this makes a lot of sense.

So what needs to be in our processes? We need structure that helps us avoid really big mistakes, what Mr. Hastings notes as processes that protect us from irrevocable disaster, such as hackers stealing customer's credit card info or producing inaccurate financials. He also goes on to observe that we need enough structure to ensure that we police our corporate character. Whether by external mandate (harassment, discrimination) or organizational mandate (dishonesty, thievery), there are characteristics of our organization that we must properly safeguard. We also need to include the design of everyday tasks using methods like Norman's cognitive engineering that is specifically geared to helping people get work done, not to control them but to empower them. That is perhaps one of the biggest challenges, as in traditional process development projects we just don't get that on our radar screen most of the time.

More from Netflix. Mr. Hastings further points out that there are good processes and there are bad processes. From his perspective, good processes might include something like Web site push every two weeks instead of randomly; and a bad process might be to get pre-approval for $5k spending. The point is that the first process is promoting an important behavior in the organization that is likely to make the company more successful. By establishing a two-week Web site push schedule, team members can plan, refine and deliver those pushes in a collaborative and highly productive manner, while producing a more predictable benefit for the company. The rule to get $5k spending pre-approved suggests oversight is required because, well, employees just are *not* responsible enough to make those kinds of decisions. Ouch, if you're an employee on the receiving end of that process it's a bit painful, isn't it? Trust?

Interestingly enough, the spending rule misses another critical level of process, the difference between working within context as compared to controlling through command. For example, if we need to trim discretionary spending to help meet our quarterly profitability goals then why wouldn't we say that? The context is clear, and gets even clearer when stated as: "We need to trim discretionary spending where possible so we can hit our quarterly profitability goals and get our bonuses." This contextual rule does not dictate specific actions out of context like the rule: "You must get pre-approval for $5k spending," though both could easily be intended to achieve the same outcome.

When we do work within context, what we find is the creation of a simplified process that in turn also simplifies the work that people need to do. A very significant part of mastering process comes from the fitness of use we deliver to the participants in the process. This is a true measure of process quality.

Process Quality (No Sigmas Allowed)

We noted the influence of Dr. Deming on process earlier in this book, but now let's talk about another quality expert that was influencing global perceptions at the same time as Deming, but from a different angle. That person was Dr. Joseph M. Juran who was concerned with quality as it applied to business and to people. Dr. Juran was also a central figure in the transformation of Japan from a military power to an economic one. Working independently of Deming, Juran focused more on management philosophies from an early stage while Deming was focusing primarily on statistical quality control.

One of the most galvanizing statements from Juran was his definition of quality – where he defined quality by its *fitness of use* for items produced and work being done with respect to the recipient of the product or work.

Dr. Juran went on to explain that quality is always judged by the receiving party regardless of what is produced. It doesn't matter if it is a tangible good, a conversation, an email, a document or anything else.

The point that Dr. Juran made when he defined quality in this way is the observation that for anything that is produced, regardless of its defect rate or adherence to a set of quality metrics, if the receiver can't easily use or consume it, then it is not a quality output.

Perhaps one of the most obvious examples comes from manufacturing where over time large manufacturers adopted MRP, MRPII and finally ERP software to help manage the sourcing, planning, scheduling, storing and shipping of materials in, and finished goods out. These software programs offered a way for organizations to gain consistent oversight on the critical, interlinked operations that manufacturing requires. Makes sense, right? Sure it does, unless you're the production floor manager.

As it turns out, these software systems (SAP, MAPICS, BPICS, JD Edwards and so on) had all the information the shop floor managers needed, but that information could not be output in a form directly useful to their work. In fact, for many years (and it's still going on in some places today) these ERP systems would output stacks of paper that the shop scheduler would then retype into a software program appropriate for actually scheduling and managing work (can you say Excel?). Sometimes this was done on a daily basis.

Over time a number of the ERP products ended up supporting the export of data in file formats that products like Lotus123 and Excel could use, although it still required adjusting the information in the spreadsheet program before it could be used to produce daily shop plans.

Now consider this. The data the shop floor needed was in the ERP system and once implemented, the ERP system commonly made more data available to the shop floor than ever before. The data was accurate, far more accurate than manual means of tracking could be. The ERP system was able to output all of the information desired every time, without errors or waiting (in most cases). So if you are creating what the next person needs with the right information at the right time without mistakes that's quality, right? Well, not exactly. While it may be better than before, if the shop scheduler has to spend hours every day to make the output usable then the output is of very low quality. As Dr. Juran said, "The user is who determines the quality of a given output."

So a big part of process design is the fitness of use as judged by managers and process participants. If their interaction with the process is not aligned to their needs, to their contexts, then the resulting process will leave them with no choice but to move outside of the process with non value-added activities to make up for the real lack of quality in the process.

In an independent research study of Gartner BPM conference attendees, survey participants were asked how often workers in their own companies designed workarounds to their business processes or systems. The 781 respondents indicated that 48.1% believed workarounds occurred *often* and 37% indicated workarounds occurred *occasionally*. From this we must understand that 4 out of every 5 process participants are finding our business process interfaces inappropriate to their needs, enough so that they at least occasionally design their own process to get their work done.

The implications of this one survey question and its responses should send chills down the spine of every business manager that sees it. Can you imagine how much opportunity we are leaving on the table in our process practices?

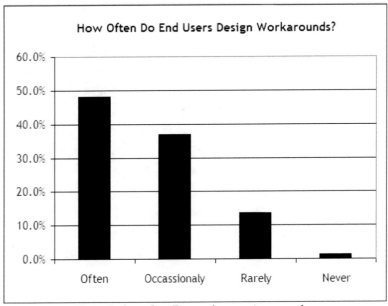

From Independent Research surveying attendees
at a Gartner BPM event in 2009 (781 respondents)

Far more important though, is the need for us to understand what we can do to mitigate these kinds of results. So what can we do?

- Can we identify who the process participants and managers are that will be expected to live with the process once it goes live? Yes.

- Can we spend time with some of them to get a sense for what would make their lives easier? Yes.
- Can we simply take the time to picture ourselves in their role, and to challenge the process as to what we would want if we had to do that work? Yes.
- Can we ask these people what their biggest headaches are, what is getting in the way of them successfully doing their jobs? Yes.
- And can we simplify the process wherever possible so there just isn't as much for them to do? You bet.

Taking the time to understand the perspectives of people who must live with the process once it goes live is a mandatory part of mastering our processes.

Personal Productivity and the iPhone?

Apple's iPhone is a hot product. Apple shipped 13.7 million iPhones in the 2008 calendar year with total units shipped over the 20 million mark as of August 2009. Sales volumes continue to grow with Apple selling 5.2 million iPhones in the second quarter of 2009, and predictions are as high as 80 million by 2012. [1]

So what's so special about the iPhone and how does it relate

---

[1] Mike Abramsky, analyst with RBC Capital Markets, predicts that the iPhone will have 5.7 percent total addressable market share by 2012 equating to a volume of over 80 million units.

to personal productivity in BPM? While for many people the connection may not be obvious for us it shouts out one of the most challenging issues in BPM.

Whether you have an iPhone or not, or you think the iPhone is really slick (or not) doesn't matter. The fact is that Apple's iPhone is dramatically easier to use than the mobile devices that preceded it, and that are trying to compete with it now. The thing is, the iPhone really is unique; not by what it can do but in how it does it. Not surprisingly, Donald Norman was an Apple Fellow in the mid-1990s where as he does now, he helps companies design products that appeal to emotions as well as reason.

Apple iPhone

Talk to an iPhone user. See how many love their iPhone. Then ask them about the instructions included with the iPhone. If you are like us, you will find that the majority of iPhone users can't even tell you about instructions because they didn't need them. The product is that easy to use.

This is the essence of what makes the iPhone so powerful, so unique and so attractive to buyers. You just use it – the computer inside disappears. Apple is not competing on features and functions; they are competing on ease of use and true simplicity. The iPhone is a shining example of what happens when we strive for sophistication as defined by Leonardo da Vinci, "Simplicity is the ultimate sophistication." Far more than just good user interface design, the iPhone provides an almost phenomenal shift in *user experience*. With the iPhone, you focus on doing what you want to do, not how to use the device. In fact, for many iPhone owners the user experience is so intuitive and simple that they are using the iPhone for far more mobile activities than ever before.

This is an order of magnitude shift in user experience and as you can probably guess, that translates directly to increased productivity. With the iPhone, many users are finding they can do more, faster than ever before.

So what would happen if our process interfaces—*the process worker experience*—was improved in this way? The answer is obvious, an order of magnitude shift in worker productivity.

Of course most of us who are working with process don't have the resources available to do this kind of inspirational development work for process that Apple had in developing the iPhone. Also, business processes have far more variation and contextual nuance than a common use device like the iPhone.

That makes the challenge even greater, yet the one thing we do have is context. We can take the context of our organization (our processes and our people) into account to aid us in developing process interfaces that are indeed intuitive, simplified and appropriate for those who do work in process. We can do our utmost to replicate the essential difference Apple made with the iPhone in the process interfaces for our process participants and process managers.

This then is indeed a critical part of increasing personal productivity. Further, if we are truly developing simplified processes, as well as simplified and intuitive process interactions, the resulting process design is far more likely to serve its intended purpose for a longer time. We are effectively minimizing the probability of process obsolescence, where with traditional band-aid process design we are maximizing the probability of process obsolescence. Given a choice, which would you choose?

With so many process implementers struggling with user-centered design it helps to see what happens when we get it *right*. What kind of results can, and should, we expect to derive from BPM? Let's look at what happened on a core process of a major automobile manufacturer when applying BPM to a subsidiary's core process.

NMAC – Orders of Magnitude Success

Nissan Motor Acceptance Corporation (NMAC) is the loan processing arm of Nissan Motors. Their core value creation process, loan processing, has a direct impact on both Nissan revenue and Nissan customer satisfaction.

Prior to using a BPM system to improve their processing performance, NMAC documented a high volume period of 40,000 applications in a one month period that required in excess of 30,000 man-hours to process. The same work volume, once the process was optimized and automated where possible within their BPM system required just over 15,000 man hours to complete.

Nissan (NMAC) – Cost Reduction with BPM Exceeding 50%

Here again we see cost reduction exceeding the 50% mark for NMAC's peak volume period, but the benefits go well beyond that. Using BPM, NMAC reduced the cost of processing loans, the processing time per loan and the elapsed time per loan. Besides cost savings, customer satisfaction was increased, which leads to a higher percentage of completed loans. That produces more car sales, and the overall positive experience increases word of mouth marketing.

Isn't that the kind of bang for our BPM buck that we are all trying to achieve?

Going further, NMAC isn't stopping there. They have already identified the next level to improve; automating the front end to eliminate low-skill, low-value prep work. From these improvements, NMAC expects to reap another 20% performance improvement driving the total performance improvement of their *core business process* to over 70%.

This case study highlights several important aspects essential to improving personal productivity. NMAC automated functions that people did not need to do and found ways to automate low-skill, low-value process activities. By doing this, they freed up their employees to do higher value work that only people can do.

But under the covers of the case study is a concerted effort to make sure user interfaces where well designed with respect to the people actually doing the work, another example of user-centered design. It's often hard to improve core processes and it is almost impossible to produce improvement results of 50% or more unless the participant interfaces are designed with participants needs in mind. That is part of the really big challenge that the vast majority of process projects just plain miss.

Missing the Target – Life in the Real World

The last piece of the personal productivity puzzle is the issue of getting "in sync" with the real world of process. Some of the actions we suggest, and certainly imply, to achieve personal productivity already cover process reality. But it is so important, and so overlooked, that it needs to be brought out on its own. The issue (opportunity) comes from the high degree of variation that occurs in the work within all processes that have significant human interaction.

Out in the trenches of process operations, many situations demand that ad-hoc actions be taken as work gets done. It's the proverbial 80/20 rule that states that 80% of the work requires handling the 20% of exceptions that arise in normal operations. Exceptions range from:

- Things that have gone missing
- Customers introducing unexpected variables
- Workloads, resource constraints, emergencies and mistakes

They all happen. If you add in pretty much anything that you can imagine that might go wrong, plus the things you can't imagine, well, that's what it's actually like in the real world of operations. Don't forget, Murphy's Law[1] remains alive and well, continuing to deliver on its promise that *anything that can go wrong will go wrong!*

This represents a real challenge for anyone designing process models because models cannot ever encode or embed all the variations that will occur in the real world.

Instead, what we must do is provide as much freedom as possible for process participants. We have to recognize, right

---

[1] Murphy's Law is most commonly attributed to Edward Murphy, an American aerospace engineer in the mid 1900s.

from the beginning, that it is impossible for us to identify all of the possible variations that can occur in human-centric processes. And we must develop user experiences that give process participants the freedom to deal with these variations.

This may seem obvious, but what we know is that the majority of process participants in our organizations are currently finding it necessary to go outside of the process experience we provide, finding their own ad-hoc ways to get things done.

Now for those who love shortcuts, we will also tell you that giving process participants the means to escalate problems is not at all a viable means for addressing this challenge. Sure, escalation can be part of our process and help in specific cases where we know something needs to be escalated. But escalation does nothing to help with the work participants *can do* that the user experience gets in the way of *doing*. The challenge is to include in the user experience ways for process participants to address ad-hoc requirements and engage with other team members when meeting new challenges. The combination of simplified user experience, flexibility to meet ad-hoc demands (freedom) and contextually relevant team collaboration can be brought together to be the holy grail of personal productivity.

Just knowing what it takes to improve personal productivity is the first step. Then we can take that knowledge into consideration for every business process we seek to improve. By including this step in our BPM approach we are another step closer to reaching our goal of true process mastery.

Step Four: Orchestrate for Real-Time Demand

It will not do to leave a live dragon out of your plans if you live near one.
—J.R.R.Tolkien in The Hobbit

One of the biggest mistakes most process initiatives make is that they leave live dragons out of the process even though those dragons are alive and well, hovering over our processes just waiting for the chance to pounce.

Of course what we mean by this is the pervasive need for organizations, people and processes to adapt on the scene to unexpected demands as they arise. This is, in essence, the orchestrating of process for real-time demand.

As you can probably imagine, this scenario is enough to drive the typical technologist stark raving mad, the engineer into the loony-bin for life and the control-freak into an early grave. *Perhaps dragon is too mild a term.*

The real challenges in orchestrating processes for real-time demand stem from the sheer number of possibilities that could occur and the fact that no matter how intensely we research, study, architect and design a process we don't have a crystal ball that can help us find every possibility. The question then becomes, if we can't design finite orchestration into the process what can we do?

What we can do is make our process design flexible in a way that gives us the capability to empower people on the front lines to adapt the process to the current context – on the fly, as it happens. While it may not be obvious how we do this, doing so addresses a number of process requirements that are otherwise handled in a very clumsy, over-engineered way.

The root cause of inflexible processes comes directly from the issue with perspectives we talked about much earlier in this book. The act of designing a process is usually tackled like a project (really, it is a project) and that tends to press us into very structured thinking. Even modeling environments do this, as they specifically give us the tools to change work routes for orchestration based on variables. In many cases we are even taught to capture the possible variations (at least the obvious ones), then encode them in the process model itself. The problem isn't that we do this; the problem comes from how we encode this process logic into our business processes.

Orchestration and Routing Variables

Most process orchestration is based on variables, thresholds and available workflow routes. Process orchestration variables are not normally accessible by supervisors and managers. But when designing process we need to think about real-time, ad-hoc, orchestration. Why wouldn't we expose orchestration variables to the people on the scene? They are the ones that have to deal with real-time variances, and they are the ones that should be in charge of making orchestration decisions.

What will they do if we don't give them the needed flexibility? Go around the system? You better believe it. How many times have you gone around the system because it was getting in your way? The truth is that if we don't empower managers to orchestrate process in real time then all we are really doing is forcing them to do so the hard way. And that hard way is something we don't have visibility into, cannot track, and are completely unable to support if something goes wrong (and it will). Exposing orchestration variables goes a long way toward helping to adapt a process against real-time demand as long as we put that capability into the hands of the managers and process participants on the scene.

So we have an orchestration model that routes orders from gold customers to the gold team, silver customers to the silver team and bronze customers to the bronze team. But suddenly we have a spike in orders from silver workers while gold orders are down. Wouldn't the manager on the scene want to change the orchestration to route silver customer orders to the gold and silver team?

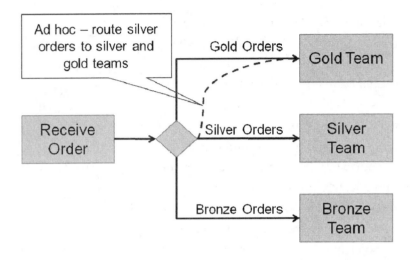

Even better, what if we had intelligent orchestration built into the process to do that for us but the manager knew to expect an influx of gold orders? Might the manager want to keep the gold team's work at a minimum in preparation for that order? How would the manager do that? They would probably have to go and tell the gold team to stop doing silver work even though the work was still coming into their work queues.

The situation may even be more complicated. It could be that the manager might then have to go to IT to get someone there to manually reverse the silver orders back out of the gold teams' work queues so that they can be rerouted to the silver team. Taking this even further, it may well be the case that the work for IT to reconcile these orders is prone to errors, causing some orders to *slip through the cracks* and not get processed.

Can you imagine how those customers might feel?

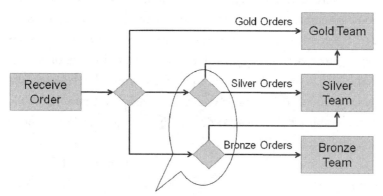

Automated Intelligent work orchestration

Yet by exposing those orchestration variables so that the manager can change process routing the model can remain directly supportive of the work that needs to be done.

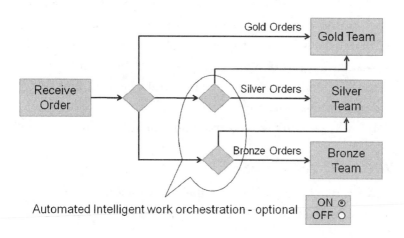

Automated Intelligent work orchestration - optional

But what happens when the variable itself is not what we need right now to orchestrate the process? Can that happen? Yes. Take for example a case where we are prioritizing our work against, let's say, loan value. We might prioritize our work by the value of each loan request we receive because of the higher value of a given work item. Let's assume that we initially build routing values based on high value loans (over $1 million) and regular loans (under $1 million).

If for some reason we suddenly had an influx of loan requests over $5 million, the manager, assuming we gave him or her access to our orchestration variables, could move the priority break to $5 million. That would enable the business to focus on the specific case of an influx of high value work that could be switched back as soon as things returned to normal.

But loan value isn't the only criterion that represents value to us. We could also have a situation where a new product line was spurring an increase in loans from existing customers who are highly likely to do even more high value business with us. Now what do we do? We don't have the right variable for our manager to orchestrate so it makes it real tough for him or her to deal with this situation.

But why couldn't we substitute one variable for another?

Variable Variables

We certainly could if that is the way we designed our process. The process engine certainly doesn't care; it's software. All it needs is the necessary set of instructions to perform its function. In fact, the concept of variables that can be changed out as needed is exactly the role a meta-model serves. The concept of meta-models is well-ingrained in software design and has been so for years.

So from the builder perspective, the process model becomes a bit more abstract. The concept of orchestration becomes one of acting on whatever variable we choose to use, with a default variable built in to handle the common case. When things change enough that the default variable doesn't meet the need, let the guy or gal on the front line plug in the one that *does* meet the need. But that does raise an interesting challenge. What are these other variables and how do we find them if we don't already know about them?

In many cases it's not difficult to come up with scenarios that would use other variables. It may only require us to look for the answer and we will find what makes sense for our processes. Other time we may interview front-line managers, getting them to talk about all the weird, wacky and incredibly frustrating things they have dealt with in the past. This is very good way to gain some insight into the scenarios we need to support.

We can also work to build feedback mechanisms so that when orchestration problems do arise we can learn from them. But maybe we can do something else. Maybe we can preemptively solve many of those challenges if we just get a bit more creative.

Expressions as Variables

In all likelihood we can actually identify what variables are indeed available to us at even given place in the process. That is our starting point as noted above, just as it was noted that we still won't cover all the possible scenarios. The biggest reason that we won't cover all of the scenarios is because a lot of them are compound scenarios.

Back to our loan process. Marketing recognized an opportunity to get some very good publicity in a geography we don't have much penetration into yet. A good impression early on is likely to give us some powerful word of mouth marketing. We should prioritize these loans. Now use an expression for orchestration that places all loan requests over $1 million and all loans from region x (regardless of value) into the priority queue. Bingo, the compound expression enables us to adapt on the fly to the orchestration needs that have just occurred.

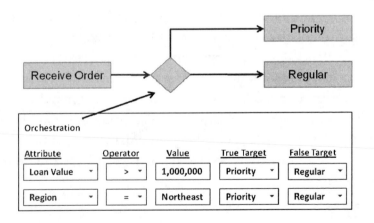

Where the magic happens is when we expose these types of orchestration capabilities as simple to use ad hoc managerial functions. If a manager can decide easily add the rule to route loans in region X to Priority while leaving the regular rule in place we have the ability to express orchestration as a compound expression.

There are knock-on effects we must consider when using real-time process orchestration, as compound expressions could have undesirable affects. In our example above, what happens if we inadvertently route the majority of incoming work to a minority of our workers? That would not be good, but that should also be the responsibility of the manager that makes the orchestration decision. For our process model, the main concern is that we don't make real-time orchestration capabilities prone to creating unwanted affects. That means we may include some orchestration guidelines, or outer boundaries, that protect from potential disaster.

Like Mr. Hastings of Netflix noted, if part of the process orchestration could result in irrevocable disaster then we should not make it accessible for change against real-time demand. Beyond that, we need to consider what happens in the real world and make our processes as flexible as possible.

Models that Miss

Another challenge in orchestrating process to real-time demand is a process model that will not allow work to be performed in a non-standard order or route. Is it possible we might have to turn a process on its head due to some external influence we didn't prepare for?

Consider this. A manufacturer receives return claims materials on Wednesday of every week. They require the paperwork for the claims to arrive 24 hours in advance.

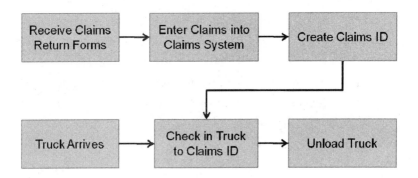

But the biggest client just completed a regional consolidation and sent the paperwork with the materials so they arrived at the same time. But our process doesn't allow us to take claims materials into receiving without the claims paperwork being processed first. This means that we don't let our biggest customer unload their return claims materials when it arrives. Sorry, that's not the way our process works.

We have the people there, so we can physically do the unloading and receiving. The space is available. The customer's truck is there, the material is in the truck, the paperwork is there but it's not *in the system* so the process won't allow us to unload and receive the goods.

This is a real story. The process couldn't be orchestrated to allow assigning the proper claims identification paperwork to the materials after receiving instead of before. The manager who was called to deal with the situation decided to unload all of the material into another warehouse across the road to keep the customer happy. Then, after the paperwork got processed, they used overtime to move all of the material back and actually receive it. In this case the manager needed the ability to change the order of the activities in process.

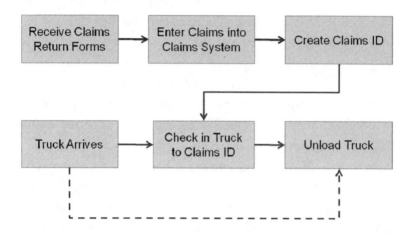

Is that something we can do in software? Of course it is. Is that really necessary? Far too often the answer is *yes* because things like this happen in the real world of process every single day.

What needs to be considered in our processes is the ability to reorder activities or even skip activities altogether when the manager with the proper authority decides this is the right thing to do.

Wait a minute, skip activities altogether? You can't be serious?

Indeed we are serious. Take for example an insurance provider that includes in their process both an initial underwriting activity and a final underwriting activity. But it just so happens that they had a surge of new business when a competitor went out of business. They didn't have the staff to cover the volume but upon review, noted that the final underwriting activity rarely impacted the quote by more than plus or minus 3%. Rather than lose the new business, the manager opted to skip the last activity only to find that the process was so tightly encoded within software that there was no way to bypass that activity and still generate the binding quote from the system.

The workaround? The only workaround they were able to find forced them to temporarily reassign a third of the claims handling department to manually reentering all of the policy information through an exception-handling interface. This meant they had to print the pre-quotes and then reenter the information from the pre-quotes into the manual binder interface. The cost of this was in excess of 10% of first year policy value (on average) but they did get the job done. What we don't know is what affects this may have had on existing customers as during a period of eight working days they ran normal operations short-staffed.

Certainly it is not the case that all processes have the need for real-time process orchestration, but far more do than we realize even if it doesn't happen often. For some processes it will never be appropriate to include this kind of process orchestration, and where it is, we will likely be required to document and track these exceptions.

Yet in many cases developing a process for the *rule* (the logical and most rationale common orchestration) that ignores the reality that exceptions will occur will often limit the value of a process. Oh, and just to make it clear, creating rigid processes that force process participants to find their own workarounds can hardly be a realistic way to think of process quality. Why would anyone think that just because we don't know those exceptions and workarounds are occurring they don't affect performance, quality, compliance and even regulatory conformance? It may be a great way to skirt around tough process challenges but under no circumstances is it great process.

Further, what about the effects on the people in the process? Can you imagine how the manager in the insurance company would have felt if he or she could have simply chosen to skip that last underwriting activity? Or the manufacturer who would have been able to receive returns normally and reconciled those returns with the paperwork on the backside? These challenges and many more are the real world of process.

Models are not process.
Software is not process.
Process is what really happens where work gets done.

By taking these truths into account we can build models and use software in ways that will truly empower the people doing the work to *get the job done.*

Step Five:
Keep Your Process in Tune

You can tune a piano, but you can't tuna fish.
—REO SpeedWagon

One of the most overlooked aspects of business process management is to keep a process in tune, aligned to achieving its intended outcome. More often than not, we are so busy running from one process to another that we don't have time to check in on processes once we complete a process project.

But processes can get out of *tune* very quickly. New requirements arise, business rules become obsolete, or some part of the context of a process changes. Though it may not happen often, sometimes processes even go out of tune while we are in the middle of the process project itself.

It's worth taking a moment to look closer at business rules. Business rules are highly prone to obsolescence because they are almost always based on context. While our context continues to change at an ever increasing rate, our rules tend to build up within processes, often locked into a reality that doesn't exist anymore.

Horse Sense

One example of an obsolete business rule is the 35-mile rule. Originating from the mid-eighteen hundreds it was considered the distance beyond which an extra charge was applied for hauling goods by horse and cart. The additional fee was for two nights stabling and inn charges incurred for travel further than a horse and cart could go in one day. This was a rule that certainly made sense for its time.

Now move that rule into the 21st century. It doesn't make any sense, does it? Yet one moving company did indeed uncover that rule buried away behind a services split that made no sense. Yes indeed, they had different services for moves under 35 miles compared to those over 35 miles.

In another case, an insurance agent for trailers and mobile homes had an internal rule that was deeply engrained in all service representatives: "Never mark a trailer insurance application as transporting live animals, no matter what." The rule existed for a reason. When it was made, the insurance agent had access to general use trailer policies only. Those policies, if the trailers were used to haul live animals, were prohibitively expensive. The agent, not wanting to lose a healthy line of business, handled the problem by instating the rule.

About five years later a new employee raised a red flag. She was doing a lot of horse trailer quotes for horse trailer policies; the horse trailer policies being a new product the agent now had available to them. This new employee asked the question: "Why am I marking all of these horse trailer policies as hauling no animals?"

Interesting question, eh? Initially, the reaction of those she queried was to restate the rule: "Never mark a trailer as hauling animals." Yet the question stuck once it was raised, making other staff wonder why they would mark horse trailers as hauling no horses.

The question did float up to the top of the organization, at which point the owner was drawn into the conversation. His reaction was predictable: "Of course we need to be marking horse trailers as hauling horses, that rule is obsolete."

The agency immediately dropped the old rule, but that is not the end of the story. Realizing that the agency had produced a significant number of horseless horse trailer policies, the staff now had to go back and update those policies appropriately. In this case, things had changed, but the old no animals rule was still there. When the new insurance products designed for hauling animals became available, the rule of marking policies as hauling no animals became obsolete.

The impact of the obsolete rule caused the agency to produce incorrect insurance policies along with a significant amount of rework to correct the effects of applying the obsolete rule.

While these examples may seem extreme, there are more obsolete rules in process than you may believe. Fortunately, we should be designing most if not all of those old rules out of the process in our design activities.

But even if we design a process void of any obsolete rules,

some of the rules in the process are highly likely to become obsolete in the future. Keeping our processes in tune requires us to identify rules and other elements of process that get skewed after we complete an improvement. If we didn't miss any obsolescence during our improvement, then we only need catch those that go out of tune after our improvement initiative is complete.

Reactive Tuning (Killing that Sour Note)

There are some relatively straightforward ways to know when a process needs a good tuning. We may see an increase in processing time, bottlenecks that arise where they didn't exist before or an increase in the number of errors generated. We may see an increase in rework or even in over time requirements for staff. We may even see an increase in customer support requests or customer complaints. These are examples of the obvious ways we know when a process is no longer aligned to our needs. They are obvious and they are painful, much like when a piano is so far out of tune that notes become sour.

But can you imagine a pianist having a piano that far out of tune? Accomplished pianists know to tune their pianos regularly, long before they can reach the point where notes turn sour. Why then would we wait until our processes have degraded to the point that we have increased processing time, bottlenecks and a sharp rise in errors or complaints? We shouldn't, of course.

What we can do is respond to change much faster by insuring that we monitor the indicators that can tell us our processes are no longer operating as before. We can catch processing time increases early on, catch bottlenecks when they are still just periodic slow downs, and jump on error trends as soon as they begin to appear. At the very least we should all do this as a matter of course. But are there other ways we can keep our processes in tune?

Protect your Gains

Symetra Financial is a group of affiliated insurance and financial services companies. The company has approximately 2 million customers, 1,200 employees, and more than $21 billion in GAAP assets. They work in partnership with over 20,000 agents and advisors providing annuities, life insurance, group employee benefits, and retirement plans throughout the U.S.

Symetra used BPM systems to handle a 67 percent increase in applications without increasing staff, actually absorbing a 14.5 percent staff attrition during a period of business growth. Case managers have each increased the number of cases they can handle by 30 percent and underwriters have increased their capacity by 20 percent. Do you think a gain like that is worth protecting?

The Symetra example includes improvement gains that are tangible and measureable. They represent very important value to the organization. They are money in the bank, so to speak. Yet many things that influence process can change, and when they do those gains can indeed be compromised.

Now, we assume you have your goals and baselines. We also assume, like Symetra, that you evaluated the results after completing an improvement project. If you did that, then you have a before and after picture that can be used to determine when gains are being compromised.

Periodically rechecking the process against the gains is just good old common sense. However, common sense doesn't seem to be all that common anymore and even the best intentions often fall to the wayside in the flurry of business activity that seems to make up our working lives. Protecting process gains requires measures we can check; with a dash of discipline to make sure we do so on a regular basis. How often do we check process gains?

Auditing theory tells us that as a pattern develops in any business activity, that pattern can be used to ramp up or down the auditing activity. If process gains remain stable over several checks, the checks can be spread out. If we catch degradation then the process needs to be checked more often. Some processes will remain stable for a long time, even many years. Others will be stable for many months and some will tend to slip in far less time. Establishing the frequency of gain checking is initially a trial and error proposition.

This is a particularly beneficial exercise considering that we are checking to insure gains we made have not been lost. There is nothing fun about fighting to win the same ground over and over again. There is also nothing fun about doing the work in the process and finding yourself in the unenviable position of struggling to meet work demand because the process became more difficult. Protecting the gains we have made is an essential part of maximizing process success. Acting to protect gains can enable us to tune our processes even faster than reactive tuning. But there is another way we can keep our processes in tune, one that can give us insight into changes before they create any significant negative impact.

Adaptation in (almost) Real Time

Change, change, change. We hear it all the time. Everything is changing. Change often starts to take place within our processes before we even complete improvement projects.

Reactive process tuning is based on identifying negative trends (e.g., backlogs, bottlenecks, significant increases in process time, and so on). These measures enable us to react to negative process trends so that we can mitigate their impact before things get to far out of hand.

Protecting gains by auditing those KPIs we used for our goals is an active means to tune processes. By auditing these critical measures we can ensure that our process retains its full value, often enabling us to capture negative impacts faster than we can with reactive process tuning.

But we can also proactively tune process by adapting our processes to changes *as they occur,* long before the effects of these changes show up in our KPIs or as negative process trends. To adapt a process to changes that occur very soon after the change takes place requires that we identify the effects of the change that has occurred. Those effects are the footprints in the sand for the root cause of what is different. The question then is, "How do we identify the effects?"

Identifying effects requires us to have measures for changing work patterns. We need to capture information about the actions people take when performing work so that we can tell when those patterns change. Such information may include:

- The number of data entry fields process participants enter data into
- The number of mistakes that get corrected as work is performed
- The number of files uploaded
- The number of documents scanned
- The number of documents accessed
- The number of forms opened

There are any number of actions that people take in a given process that are likely to follow a pattern that can be tracked. Changes to patterns tell us that something in, or around, the process had changed; and they tell us where to look for the root cause of the change.

This practice can reveal many things about a process. It can prove or disapprove our assumptions about how work gets done. When we give process participants an interface into the process, it should fit them in a certain way based on what we think we know about how they work. But if we are able to measure many of those aspects, we can quickly identify places where we were wrong.

This helps us quickly adapt to mistaken assumptions and capitalize on opportunities. Where we fall short of our expectations, we can adapt the process while also learning what doesn't work, just as we will learn what does work so that we can leverage that knowledge in the future.

Beyond that initial stage, tracking action patterns will quickly tells us when things change, allowing a more proactive response to change. Using pattern checking also filters out the noise of one-off bumps and bounces so that we don't react to false alarms. This is about the most proactive we can get in identifying change, and it is far beyond what most of us do now. Setting up adaptive measures and analysis views does take more work, but perhaps it only seems like more work. Maybe the only real issue is how we think of process. For example, how would things change if we thought about our processes as gardens?

TLC for Process

Like a garden, processes do need tender loving care. We must oversee them; pulling the weeds and pruning away the dead growth. As with gardening, when we do this it requires less work on a more regular basis as compared the much larger effort required once things have gotten out of hand.

The results are more positive as well. A garden that is tended on a regular basis looks attractive almost all of the time.

A process that is tended regularly functions effectively almost all of time. By investing smaller amounts of time on a regular basis, we are able to keep our processes in tip-top shape and have far fewer major projects that we have to do.

When we change our perspective on process in this way our behavior toward our processes also changes significantly. It becomes habit to catch issues early on and nip them in the bud before they become real problems. We can only do this with adaptive improvement. That means we need to monitor as many patterns as we can.

With the three ways of keeping our processes updated and in tune (reactive, active and proactive) we can protect the gains we have made and ensure our organization reaps the full benefits of our labors.

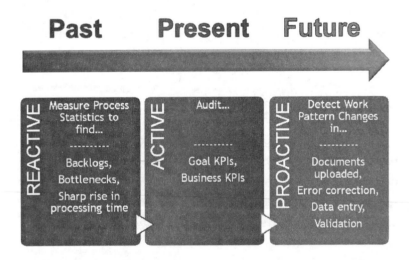

Depending on our circumstances, we may start with reactive processing tuning or by actively protecting gains. But no matter where we start, our goal should be to work our way to the inclusion of adaptive tuning in our practice when we can. Keeping our processes in tune will ensure that we continue to optimize how work gets done. Like the professional pianist, process masters pay close attention to their processes to ensure they remain operating at peak efficiency.

Step Six: Create Transparency

Sometimes you make the right decision; sometimes you make the decision right. —Dr.Phil

It is far easier to make a right decision that it is to make a decision right. In these days of the information age, we are awash with information we can use in the decision-making process. The challenge is not in finding information – it is in finding the right information needed to support good decision-making.

Most astute people can, when given relevant information, logically and rationally make a decision that seems right. Many such decisions are defensible, meaning that the analysis of the information available is highly likely to validate such decisions. Yet that doesn't mean it is a good decision, and it doesn't mean the decision was made in the right way.

Rapid Cognition

In 2005, a book was published that took the business world by storm. It sparked controversy and rebuttal while getting rave reviews and almost fanatical word of mouth publicity. The book was *Blink*, by Malcolm Gladwell and it tells the story of rapid cognition.

Rapid cognition is concerned with the ability of the human mind to make very quick decisions based on a small set of salient facts. There are two prerequisites to *blinking* something: "Limited but relevant information and acting on the conclusion that leaps to mind almost instantly when presented with this kind of information."

Blink is a book that provides very clear and compelling examples of how our snap judgments, instincts, and gut feelings can often serve us better than rigorous decision-making behaviors. Whether you believe you blink things better than you think them, there are two takeaways that are very important from the observations that Gladwell makes in his book. First, we are indeed far more likely to make the right decisions if we have the right information at hand. That does not mean having the right information mixed in with information we don't need; and it does not mean having information in a form we have to convert before it becomes relevant to the decision at hand.

Second, whether we choose to agree with Gladwell that a blinking decision is a better way to be right more often or not, we all know that some decisions are easy to make with confidence if we have the right set of facts at hand. These are the two magic ingredients for process decision-making, but they cannot exist without process transparency.

Critical Oversight and KPIs

In the first step to mastering our processes we discussed the importance of creating KPIs as the means to manage our processes to reach their goals. Those goals may come from different motivations, but we can still build KPIs to focus our efforts and validate our success. When we talked about adapting processes to real-time demands we noted active measures for process. The KPIs used in setting goals are part of our active measurement set.

Most process KPIs need to be described at a high level then broken down to actual process data. Transparency is best achieved by defining process KPIs at the highest level first. Such KPIs could include things like:

- Total process cost and average cost per unit
- Total volume transacted, and the relationship to norms and targets
- Revenue generated, again presented against established norms and targets

Information and decisions that KPIs back will often be driven by the perspectives of individual managers. For example, the COO perspective is often one of broad performance measures around operational performance and productivity (Balanced Scorecard). The CFO is likely to be concerned with a view of process that relates information to financial performance (ROI). Sales managers are likely looking for lead and deal flow. Service managers may be looking at transacted volumes, cycle times, queues and dispositions. Quality managers may be looking for defect rates, rework, and error statistics.

Yet all of these KPIs derive from basic process measures we can capture, usually done so with BPM system software. These measures are the backbone of process transparency and are a critical factor in mastering our processes.

Process Metrics: Understanding the "Box"

Processes have a start and a finish (at least most do). Thinking of process as a black box, something (work) goes into the box and at some point exits the box. Exiting the box means the work item is no longer in the process – instead it is a completed transaction or interaction.

For transactions we can measure volume as counts for whatever time period we specify. Counts can include what went into the process and what went out of the process, again for any time period we choose. We can also relate these counts to norms, averages and targets.

We may also have multiple exits from a process, and we can track that as well. The same applies for work that enters a process. We may also care where work came from and where it is going to in those cases where work can enter a process from multiple paths (other processes). Where multiple process exits exist, we may care about the paths work may follow that lead to these exits. Often times these routing choices are based on the condition of one of more work attributes that we can also track by value.

We can track volume by attribute. If we have green, red and blue work items we can slice counts into the categories of red, green and blue item counts. Time can be tracked starting with when a work item went into the box, and when it came out. That is the elapsed time for a work item. Touch time can be measured, which is the aggregate of time spent actually working on item while it is in the box.

Routing may also be of importance. Work items can take different routes inside the box, depending on any number of conditions used to orchestrate a process. We can capture the routing path of a work item through the box. This could include dispositions, such as sales leads that covert to actual sales versus ones that do not. In the case of sales, the sales process may have several points in the process where a branch in the route is terminal [1] – ending work on the item.

For work that is in the box, we can track work items at each activity or step of the process (commonly called queues and work in progress) for an overview of what is being worked on and what is waiting to be worked on.

All of these measures are available to us regardless of the type of process we are dealing with. They are common process measures used to build informational views based on the needs of process participants and process managers.

We noted earlier that creating KPIs for process transparency starts at the top, and works down. The process metrics we just discussed sit toward the bottom of the taxonomy. We discuss them now because understanding what can be measured is important in the upcoming discussion on creating those high-level KPIs and process transparency. Now, before we switch back to the high-level KPIs we need to drop down one more level to metrics inside the box.

Process Metrics inside the Box

Once we are inside the box, we find a number of things. We will have the activities, or steps, of the process that are where the majority of process participant work gets done. We may

---

[1] Terminal routes in a process, depending on how the process is modeled, can produce a result that makes it appear work items never leave "the box." This is not a problem but it may require a slightly different reconciliation for some process metrics.

also have sub-processes. Ideally, sub-processes are mini-processes in their own right. They have one or more entrances, activities, workflow and one or more exits.

Many process participants work in just one or a few activities of a process. It really depends a lot on what work is being done, how the process is shaped (or designed) and how each organization has organized itself around getting work done. In some cases, process participants may work in many activities.

There is information we can track for each activity or step whether it is in a process or sub-process. That information is very similar to what we can track for a process (or box). We can track elapsed time starting when work enters the activity's queue, and the exit time. We can also measure touch time, counts per unit of time, number of errors, routing results where work items can exit a process and go to different places in the process workflow. We can measure these things against work item attributes. All in all, activities pose essentially the same set of metrics as we have for a process, with the process metrics being an aggregated view of multiple activities.

You should be starting to pick up a pattern here, because a pattern does exist and that pattern is what we can use to connect process metrics between levels, or perspectives, on processes. If the pattern didn't exist, we would have to create that connection for everything and that is an endeavor not worth even contemplating (let alone doing). Can you imagine what would happen if we did that?

Process Powered Transparency

Process-powered transparency uses the metrics we have already discussed by adding in context and aggregated metrics to form different perspectives. We don't have to start at the top, but it's generally easier if we do

Actually, it's probably a bit easier to start one level below the very top, which is the C-level view of the organization. Rolling processes up leads to a set of major process areas, and it is typically easier for us to work with transparency at this level first. Often this is one step or level below the C-level view or highest view of process.

When we start to work with major process areas, we are looking for a set of naturally occurring break points that exist in most organizations – sales, marketing, manufacturing, logistics, customer service, human resources and accounting. They form the natural break points we are looking for. Obviously, all of these groups have relationships to other groups in the organization, but in most cases there is a natural separation.

For example, let's start with sales. At the highest level of sales, managers need to see an aggregate of sales activities that include things like the number of sales, financial value, win-loss ratio, segregation by region, and so on.

If we have sales processes in place, that should be easy to reflect. This is the information we can track for sales processes, only it's an aggregated view across the entire organization. Summary sales information, if presented correctly, can give the sales executive the ability to "blink" an understanding of the operational state of the sales organization. If everything is fine, then the decision is that no action is required. If something is amiss, the blink-like decision will often be one of recognizing an action that must be taken.

The thing is, if the appropriate and intuitive view is presented to the sales executive, that view will empower the executive to immediately recognize when something is different than expected. Whether good or bad, deviation from the expected or normal pattern means we need to understand what has changed. Now, if the view presented is good enough that the sales executive can blink the fact that *something* has changed, that almost always means it's easy to identify *what* has changed. Now all that needs to be done is a bit of exploration as to *why* it has changed.

If sales are up in one region above forecast or history, we want to know *why*. Knowing why can help us to leverage the difference in other areas, just as it can help us address issues if sales are below forecast.

Now let's look into an example from operations. Assume that we are behind in processing loan applications and a backlog is starting to grow. Let's also assume that loan processing moves through three functional areas; application processing, dupe check and validation. As we mentioned earlier, a process gives us the ability to track counts, queues, time and dispositions. At the highest level we might see the aggregate of loan processing presented as something as simplistic as a graph showing volumes and processing times.

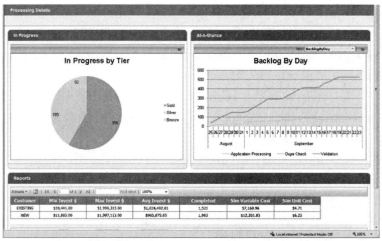

Process Dashboard – Loan Application Process Data

In the dashboard view above we can see that our work item backlog by day is on a marked upward trend. At a glance the limited by highly relevant information presented here lets a manager know something is different – and it is the process backlog. The combination of presenting selected relevant information within the context of the manager enables rapid cognition to occur.

In some cases this is all the information a higher-level manager may feel the need to know. A common action in a case like this would be to initiate a query to managers at the next level down in the organizational hierarchy. This is an important point. The dashboard presented here is very simple, enabling managers to quickly formulate actions.

Let's look at the view of the manager who is a degree closer to where work is being done by zeroing in on one aspect of the dashboard. This manager, who is responsible for loan applications, needs to know more than just that a backlog exists. This manager needs to know the *source* of the backlog.

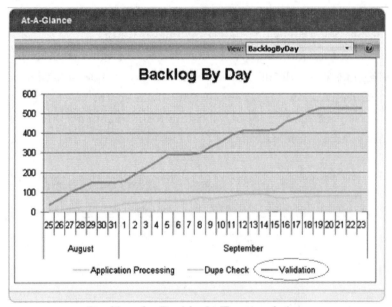

Dashboard – Backlog by Functional Area

The dashboard display here clearly shows that the queue backlog is in the validation area. Knowing the backlog is in validation, the manager can quickly query the validation supervisor to find out what is causing the backlog.

As we move through the rest of this example, we want to observe what is actually happening. The higher the view of process, the more process data is aggregated. All views derive from the same process data; it's really just a matter of understanding the perspective. As we move down from a higher level, we are drilling deeper into process data. That means that we can also provide access to lower, more detailed, views from a higher level for managers at the click of a button if that is desirable. Sometimes it is, and sometimes it is not.

The validation supervisor has a view into the process that provides more detailed process information inside *the box*. This perspective now brings things into much sharper focus, as we can see that in activity of validating loan documents, Step 1 is the source of the backlog.

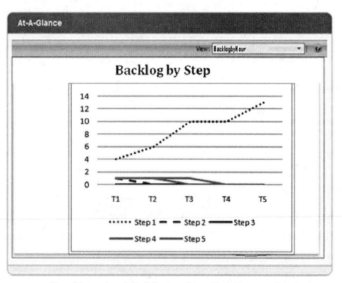

Dashboard – Validation Detailed Queue Analysis

At this point the supervisor has a very clear understanding of where things have gone awry. But there is still no insight into what has changed. There is only the insight that something has changed in the first step of the validation department's part of the process

The supervisor, knowing where the problem is, heads out to the group that validates loan documents to find the root cause of the problem. After just a couple minutes of conversation, the supervisor understands that a number of the loan documents are coming through very dark from the scanning operation in processing. They are so dark that validation has been taking the extra step of retrieving the original documents and rescanning them.

The supervisor also finds out that the problem has been going on for about six weeks, but was far worse when staff arrived for work this morning. He also finds that a service request was issued to processing to help fix the situation.

Upon meeting with the supervisor for processing, they compare notes with neither having been aware of the problem until now. Further research shows the request from validation was received by processing who then entered an IT maintenance request. Even further digging showed that IT had issued a service request to the scanner service provider who had a service call scheduled for next week.

An emergency request brought a scanner service technician out who changed out the old unit with a new one to get the process back up quickly to speed.

So why did we bother to tell you all of that detail? Well, it's kind of an interesting story and a good bit fun to tell. But that's not why we told it.

There are two important takeaways from this example. First is the chain of casualty that we followed from a very high level down to the specific process step where the root cause of the problem existed. This is a demonstration of the power of a *transparent* process that can be achieved when process data is tracked and properly aggregated to higher level views.

The second connects back to our discussion on keeping our processes in tune. Do you remember when we talked about adaptation in real time? If we had adaptive change mechanisms in place what would have happened in this scenario?

Obviously the people in validation were doing more work. They were scanning in documents, something they do not normally do. Adaptive improvement would *note the increase in document uploads in the validation department at Step 1- a process step that does not normally include the uploading of documents*, enabling us to catch this before a backlog could raise red flags. The supervisor for validation would have had *visibility* into the fact that his/her staff were suddenly scanning documents daily when they had rarely scanned documents before at all.

We've discussed the process metrics that can be tracked at the process and activity level. We've demonstrated how those metrics can be rolled up into higher level views, aggregating more and more process data the higher we go.

Those higher level views will often have their own KPIs. At

the highest level or perspective of the organization, the C-level, we would typically see an aggregate of the major process areas and results against major area KPIs.

This is process transparency. It all starts with tracking process metrics. It comes alive by aggregating, consolidating, and simplifying process metrics into views that are contextually relevant to the viewer. It includes KPIs that roll all the way to the C-level.

A gazillion reports or terabytes of data won't make anything transparent. Contextually irrelevant presentation of data won't make anything transparent.

Only when we use the real data at hand, and use it in the right way for the right reasons, can managers hope to be able to make the right decisions right. That is how to master process transparency.

Personal Analytics

But wait a minute. We are not quite finished yet. The last mile in process transparency requires us to go back down into the trenches where the real work of process gets done.

With KPIs from major process groups defined, we can create transparency up to the C-level. We can also drill down into process all the way to the activity level of a sub-process.

When we set goals for our KPIs more powerful transparency techniques becomes available. We can now drill down through our process hierarchy with goals to build personalized goal metrics explicitly aligned to the organization's KPIs.

Back to our loan application example, if we had a goal to complete all loan applications in 4 hours or less we could parse that 4 hours down into sub-goals at the process level (customer accounts, processing and underwriting). Whatever the sub-goals are, they obviously must aggregate to 4 hours or less to meet our goal. For example, if a specific activity such as validation needed to be completed in 1 hour, we should manage that part of the process by a 1 hour KPI.

We can further parse that down to the activity level knowing that the sum of activity goals needs to equal the next higher goal. In other words, the sum of activity goals for processing must equal the overall processing goal. For example, if step 1 of validation then we might give the process participants that perform the work in step 1 a view into their personal analytics like that shown here. Drilling down from KPIs gives us the ability to create personal analytics explicitly linked to organizational KPIs.

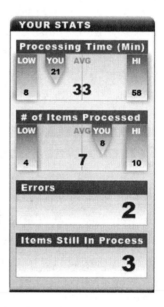

But what is missing from this from the perspective of the process participant? They know what the goal is (33 minutes) and they know what their results are in respect to that goal. But what they don't know is why this goal matters, right?

Do you remember as a child ever being told by your parents to do something, and when you asked *why* you had to do that, you were told *because we said so*? How did you feel? Like a child? How did that affect our motivation?

Motivation is directly tied to purpose and understanding. When people know why something is important, instead of just knowing that it is important, they become motivated to do the right things for the right reason.

Now, if we include the reason why a given process goal exists (in our case the goal of processing all loan applications in 4 hours or less) we have both goal and KPI transparency within context. The result might be something like:

This is illustrates another level of transparency that is driven down into the organization rather than the transparency we first discussed that was rolled up in the organization.

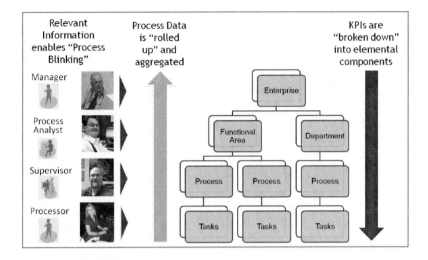

Using both rolled up and driven-down process metrics and goals creates bidirectional transparency that will bring the organization into alignment no matter how large or complex it may be. As long as relevant information is presented in context, this use of transparency will enable the organization to work in unity towards the same set of goals, with the same set of measures.

Step Seven: Design, Manage and Deliver the Customer Experience

If you do build a great experience, customers tell each other about that. Word of mouth is very powerful. —Jeff Bezos

If you build a *poor customer experience*, you can bet that even more of your customers will tell each other about that.

Word of mouth is indeed powerful but it is not always in our favor. Much depends on our ability to design, manage and deliver on a specific, desirable, customer experience.

So what does this have to do with business process management you might ask?

About the book *Customer Expectation Management: Success Without Exception*, Colin-Coulson Thomas, Professor of Direction and Leadership at the University of Lincoln wrote, "The book makes an explicit connection between customer experience and business process management. Yet this remains an area that we still haven't taken on in the BPM industry by-in-large; though it is starting to surface in more and more conversations – finally."

Customer expectations can have a lot to do with BPM,

enough so there is entire book on the subject - *Customer Expectation Management: Success Without Exception.*

Let's consider the case of a business that is really struggling with shrinking profits and falling revenues. There are lots of things businesses facing these challenges could do. They could implement cost-cutting strategies or reengineer processes. They could even reorganize or change the management team. This is the kind of reaction we often see when a business has an *internal* focus. It looks internally to see how it can reshape, reorganize, re-prioritize or re-implement new controls that appear to be addressing the problem the company faces.

Yet these actions are focused only the symptoms of a much deeper problem that is rooted in the customer experience they have been delivering. Part of the challenge is that the delivering experiences that delight requires an external or *outside-in* view of the organization. It's not something that can be found from the inside-out perspective.

An outside-in view may surface in practices such as the *voice of the customer*, but that still falls far short of addressing the complete customer experience. While voice of the customer methods attempt to bring the perspective of the customer into the internal discussion, the customer experience sits completely outside the organization. The customer experience is owned by the customer, not by the business. Whether we like it or not, the customer is the judge, jury and sometimes executioner when it comes to assessing the customer experience that any business delivers.

Many companies struggle with the inability to reorient themselves to the customer experience leaving them no choice but to act solely within the constraints of the internal view. It's not uncommon for organizations under pressure to shuffle any number of internal aspects of the business, but what good does it do to shuffle the chairs on the deck of the Titanic?

Not much. Only by recognizing and addressing the root cause of the problem, which is more often than not the customer experience, can organizations stave off disaster.

Looking into this concept of internal versus external perspectives a bit further, we can note some traditional thinking that is characteristic of internally focused organizations. We've all dealt with internally focused companies before, and they are still very much a part of our world. Although they *promise* to deliver value to their customers even without walking in their customers' shoes, playing the promise game is a very dangerous tactic indeed.

The Promise game

The promise game is all about marketing, or perhaps it is better to say it is all about emotional marketing. Promise marketing always promises something, and suggests that what you will get is better than what you could get anywhere else. The downside of promise marketing is that it usually doesn't focus on real customer value. Even more dangerous is the aspect of promise marketing that suggests, insinuates or implies some-

---

[1] Cartoons; Art by Christy Schurter, digitized by Alex Morse

thing the company or product *cannot deliver*. There is nothing that will send customers away faster than making promises that the company or product cannot, or has no intention to, actually deliver.

One example comes from the wireless U.S. telecommunications companies. These organizations are heavily engaged in promising marketing, often focusing their promise marketing with respect to the promises of their competitors. This is the old—*why we are better than the other guys* syndrome, and it results in messages like:

- More strong-signal bars!
- It's *the* network!
- More strong-signal bars in more places!
- Herds of people following you!

The cartoon contrasts the results of Virgin Mobile USA's meteoric rise in customer acquisition (5 million in 5 years) at a time when wireless Telcos Verizon, Cingular and ATT were plagued with defections due to very poor customer service. The promise from Virgin Mobile was no contracts, no hassles; a promise that Virgin Mobile can and did keep.

For those of you who don't remember, it was only a few years ago that many people were averaging over 30 minutes in the *process* of signing-up for new service with the tier-1 wireless Telcos. Some of these companies even took the onerous step of segregated in-store queues for existing customers and new customers. Can you guess which lines were the longest? If you guessed *new customers* then you need to guess again.

But the point of this step in process mastery is to help you design, manage and deliver on the customer experience. While looking at examples of companies that are very poor at doing that helps to show us what not to do; it doesn't help to show us what we should do.

The Customer Experience

Great insight about the customer experience comes from Dr. Juran when he challenged management thinking with his perspective on quality. Clearly the first management leader to bring customer expectations into management philosophy, he considered "fitness of use," applied to either goods or services to be the critical factor in successful management.

Dr. Juran asserted that meeting customer expectations is the most important strategic activity for a commercial organization. He argued that the expectations are set by understanding fitness of use and that they are fulfilled by consistently delivering on those expectations (quality).

How often do we see businesses that violate this concept on a regular basis? Look around, it's happening ever day. The reason why the Apple iPhone is experiencing such phenomenal success is that it is simple and fun to use, just as it is powerful and highly flexible. By giving customers a very intuitive user experience along with lots of very compelling features and functions Apple has hit the fitness-of-use nail on the head. While competitors talk about all of the things their products can do, and how easy it is to use them, Apple is busy actually delivering on the promise.

Have you heard of a company called Discount Tire? Depending on how old you are, buying tires for your automobile may illicit memories of frustration, anger and general distrust. That was the nature of the automobile tire market when companies like Sears, Montgomery Wards, and others used up-sell strategies and charged for every possible "service" you can imagine.

Then along came Discount Tire with a completely different business proposition. Offering quality tires at a reasonable price, great customer service, no up-selling and few additional services they reshaped the tire market in their own image.

Every customer experience is made up of the aggregate of the customer's interactions with the business, their expectations before entering into the interactions (e.g., a 10-minute oil change means it takes 10 minutes) and the resulting outcomes at the end of the process. The expectation for tires is simple. If you advertise tire prices, they should be decent tires, you should have them in stock, and the customer shouldn't be expected to pay much more than what was advertised. Before Discount Tire, the business approach was to lure people in with low prices and then work them to at least double the price point. That was the way it was until Discount Tire came along.

Founded in 1960 by Bruce T. Halle with six sets of tires (four of them recapped), this privately held company now books over $1.5 billion in revenue per year. In a crowded market of big chains and long-established tire service centers, Discount Tire has risen to be the undisputed king of the retail tire industry. How did Discount Tire do it?

Discount Tire followed an extremely simple principle of simplifying the customer experience while meeting the customer expectation the company set in the marketplace. Good tires, fair prices, no up-sell, and limited extra services that are the customer's choice. In fact, Discount Tire gives away the most common non-choice service; they fix flat tires for free.

Virgin Mobile, Apple and Discount Tire are great examples

of what the customer experience should be and what it can do for companies when they use it to simplify and satisfy customer needs. But how do we go about including the customer experience in our processes, particularly the ones that aren't as much about the overall value proposition of the company but instead support the many, varied interactions we have with our customers each and every day?

Moments of Truth

Business professor and management consultant, Richard Norman pioneered the idea of *moments of truth* as a management tool. His insights into customer value creation, value creation systems, moments of truth and more reach into every nook and cranny of an organization's operations. Introducing the metaphor of moments of truth to the business world in the 1970's, Norman presented the fundamental concepts of that are the foundation for thinking about the customer experience today.

Jan Carlzon, CEO of the Scandinavian Airlines System (SAS) popularized Norman's philosophy on moments of truth when he used the principles as the rallying points in his turnaround of SAS in the early 1980's. Following the dramatic turnaround of SAS with Carlzon at the helm ($17 million loss in 1981 to a $54 million profit in 1982), Carlzon penned his perspective and insights into his book *Moments of Truth*.

Many of the more practical elements of managing moments of truth are woven into the Carlzon-SAS story. Recognizing that people (not systems or rules) on the front-lines are the only place potential Moments of Misery can be transformed to Moments of Magic, Carlzon flipped the organizational chart from an operational perspective moving decision-making responsibility directly to the people dealing with customers and away from their managers.

Presenting a powerful case for the value of doing the right things (not just doing things right), Carlzon championed the customer focus then decentralized and reordered authority, triggered a wave of morale boosts that further improved the organization's success.

For mastering our processes, we can use moments of truth as an analysis mechanism to document customer experiences and then improve them. Where we earlier stated that the customer experience is the aggregate of the customer's interaction with us we can now make that actionable by recognizing that any interaction the customer has in a process is a Moment of Truth.

Mapping the Customer Experience

The customer experience is a process, the process the customer experiences from his or her point of view. It's quite easy to identify with the customer process because we are all customers, and if we just take a moment to think about a given process as if we were the customer we can understand where it starts, and where it ends. We can also identify moments of truth along the way as customers interact with the process. Moments of truth exist anywhere the customer touches the process. That includes Web site interactions, phone calls, mail, email, in person conversations, and so on. By thinking about being a customer in the process it's not hard to identify each of these touch-points.

Moments of truth also tell us what internal processes impact the customer experience. More often than not, customer experiences will span multiple internal processes and functional areas. Yet even under this condition we can take action once we map the internal processes to the customer experience. That is the bridge to really owning the customer experience, and it starts with designing the experience we want to deliver, then shaping how our internal processes can be rendered to meet customer expectations, not the other way around where we can cause the customer to cope with our internal processes. In other words, we should map the internal process model to the customer's mental model.

Designing the Customer Experience

Moments of truth give us the great insight into the customer experience. Once these are documented we will have a solid understanding of what the customer actually experiences with us now.

Then the questions become: "Is this what we desire for them to experience? Is this their desired experience?" But before we answer these questions, we need to look a bit deeper into what the current experience really means to the customer.

We do that by documenting what the customer wants to achieve, their desired outcomes. As a customer, if we are trying to update our personal information, buy a product, change a service, or are seeking support for a problem we certainly have an outcome in mind. Knowing that outcome, we can then review the customer experience to see if what we do now is aligned to that outcome. It is important to remember that the customer only sees the process from his or her perspective. It is the only perspective that matters.

So are we providing the right experience? Is it happening quickly enough? Is it simple and direct? If we were the customer, is the experience our company provides something we would feel meets our expectations?

In more cases than not, the answer to at least some of these questions is no. We can, however, design the customer experience by contrasting what the experience is now with what it should be, again by challenging the process as if we were the customer. We can also look at the Moments of Misery in the process and challenge them to envision Moments of Magic, dramatically increasing the quality of the customer process. This is what Carlzon did to achieve the SAS turnaround.

Once we have completed designing the customer experience (what we want to deliver) the next step is to build the means to manage it.

Managing the Customer Experience

We can't manage the customer experience if we don't have the means to measure what we are doing. It is imperative that we identify what we will measure, how we will measure it and how we will judge our success. We do this for each of the customer touch points in our processes.

For example, if we believe a product request (such as for a loan or insurance policy) should be processed in 24 hours or less, then that is one of our customer experience goals. More subtly, if we believe that the customer should only have to talk to one person, then that too becomes part of our customer experience Balanced Scorecard goals. For support requests it can get a bit tricky, as we may have a goal of giving the answer the customer needs the first time. In this case we will have to be more creative in how we measure our delivery.

Finally, we need to go back to our mapping work and sort out how our internal processes fit into our measures and goals for the customer experience. Remember that the customer experience likely spans multiple internal processes and functional areas. Because of that, we need to break out measures and goals as they apply to each area of the business. If we do this right, the end result is that we will also meet our overall customer experience goals.

Delivery on the customer experience might seem to be simple once we have our goals identified and broken out by internal process or functional area. But that, in itself, won't get us there. As we just discussed, we need to make sure we have our measurements in place so that we can track our success against our goals. But we need to be careful here. Just giving goals to people without context can disconnect them from why those goals are important. So we need to be very careful that we are measuring the right things.

One example is the big push on *one call* for call centers in the early 2000's. If our goal is to get the customer the answer they need in one phone call, then tracking call dispositions might be one of our measures. But handling a customer contact in one phone call does not mean we actually gave them the answer they wanted. By providing the context that we are committed to providing customers the answer they *want* in one call, we make it clear what we are trying to achieve. How could we measure if we are giving our customers the answers they seek? We can record these customer conversations and review them. While we may not be able to review all of them, we can certainly develop an auditing program that keeps us on target. Or we can ask customers to complete a 20-second satisfaction survey after the call.

To better assist our front-line staff that are dealing with our customers, we should produce a very clear summary of the customer experience that we are committed to delivering. Having the customer experience goals clearly stated can motivate and enthuse the employees we rely on to deliver that experience. After all, we are all customers and know what we expect as customers. We also desire to do good things thereby ensuring our self-worth and our value). If we understand the positive value we are delivering to our customers in our processes we will take ownership of the customer experience, and we will work hard to deliver experiences that delight.

Summarizing the Insiders' Insights

You may not use all of the seven steps in everything you do. It may be hard to put some steps to work for you right now. But nobody gets it right all of the time and using any of the steps will definitely increase the success of your process efforts.

These seven steps are the foundation for designing and managing great processes. But they are also the means to a transformational end that far exceeds the value that can be derived from any one process. A given company typically has 10-15 major business processes and hundreds or thousands of sub-processes. By striving to become a process-managed enterprise, process mastery can be the key to transforming your organization into an adaptive and agile enterprise that can thrive in the midst all manner of change.

In the book *The Tipping Point*, Malcolm Gladwell explores the factors that lead to dramatic change. What Gladwell uncovers is that rapid adaptation occurs when two things come together. First there must be pressure, a common frustration with the way things are now. Organizations that struggle with business and economic challenges are fraught with this kind of frustration. Sooner or later they reach the point where enough is enough.

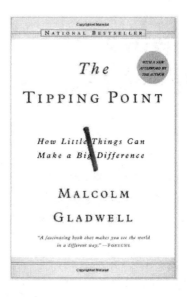

That point, the tipping point, is when dramatic change can start to happen. But it won't happen by itself. Besides the need to change, another element is needed. A triggering event must occur. As Gladwell points out, that trigger often comes from a small group that does what is right, for the right reasons. When an organization reaches a tipping point and someone steps up to the plate by doing the right thing, it's like putting a match to dry kindling; then the flame of change bursts into life and spreads like a wild fire. It burns through all of the deadwood and bramble as we rapidly shift to a new paradigm that eliminates the very source of our frustrations.

Process masters are often the ones to strike the match that lights that fire. They challenge the status quo, pressing their organizations to do the right things, not just do things right. Their results are what we all yearn for, and their processes change our lives for the better by aligning everything we can to how work really gets done—*one process at a time.*

Seven Steps Summarized

As a quick reference and review guide, this chapter summarizes each of the seven steps. It is easy to refer back to specific sections of the book for any step; each step is its own chapter and the chapter title is the name of step.

Step One – Understand and Embrace your Goal

1. Identify what needs to change.
2. Translate that need to a goal.
3. Identify metrics for measuring the goal.
4. Measure them now, to establish the baseline.
5. Set the target, thereby defining success.
6. Use your metrics to assess your ongoing success.
7. Learn from the results.
8. Continually improve your goal setting skills.

When we work with process we seek to achieve something. We have *motivation*; otherwise we wouldn't be doing anything to begin with. That motivation, whatever it may be, is what shapes our goals but we can't leverage those goals unless we make them formal goals.

Formal goals include one or more measures, a baseline and

an analysis of results after implementation. We need to identify what we can measure in the process that accurately reflects our goals, take measurements now to create our baseline, and take measurements after we have implemented our process initiative to assess our success over time.

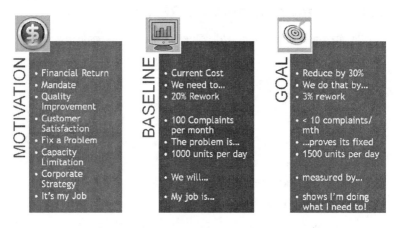

Our goals may be financial goals based on an ROI analysis. They can also be based on a set of KPIs that represent what we want to achieve or what is undesirable about the current process. In either way, KPIs must be measurable; we must establish our baseline; and we must assess our success after our improvement efforts are complete.

KPIs can also be used for the customer experience, focusing our efforts on the process from the perspective of our customers and what they actually experience with us.

Step Two – Build an Elegant Design

1. Start with the high-level process model.
2. Build your own goals if they aren't there already.
3. Optimize the high-level model to goals; the *to be* process.
4. Build the executable process behind the *to be* process.
5. Seek simplicity; it is the key to success.
6. Identify white-space.
7. Automate to minimize impacts of white-space.
8. Don't make people do what software can.
9. Don't try to make software do what people must.
10. Be wary of orchestration; tightly constrained orchestration will often impose rules that are not realistic.
11. Simplify the user experience. Without this, our best laid plans may fall to ruin.

In building an elegant process design we begin with the high-level process model. Using a very simple *as is* model, we challenge the process against our goals to help us design the best high-level *to be* process we can. If we don't have process goals in place, we use the high-level model and process stakeholder concerns to craft our goals.

From the high-level *to be* process, we craft the executable process making sure that we eliminate as many process hand-offs in the white-space as possible. We automate the things that people do not need to do wherever possible. But we also avoid automating those things people need to do. Instead, we look to optimize those human tasks through automation that simplifies the work people must do.

In all cases we continually challenge ourselves to achieve the goal of simplification.

Further, we avoid constrictive process orchestration and seek ways to put orchestration in the hands of the managers *on the scene*.

Finally, we recognize that the people who do the work, the participants in the process, are at the center of our design work. The only way we can expect people to be successful in doing the work of process is if we design it with them in mind.

Step Three – Improve Personal Productivity

1. Design Experiences, not just Interfaces.
2. Strike a Balance between People and Process.
3. Work within the User's Context.
4. Practice "Fitness of Use" as Defined by Dr. Juran.
5. Make everything as Simple as Possible.
6. Make everything as Flexible as Possible.
7. Less is more.

The most difficult part of improving personal productivity is the challenge to design experiences, not just interfaces. That's what Apple did with the iPhone and that is what we must do to the very best of our abilities.

Remember that people who work in process are people. Treat them like people, and recognize that the more rigid the process design is, the more challenging it will be for people to work with it. Read Donald Norma's book, *The Design of Every-day Things*, then keep it on your bookshelf for reference.

Don't forget that personal productivity exists within the context of the user, not the designer. Process participants have to live with the process interfaces we supply them, as well as all of the other influences around them. Our software is only part of the process they are engaged in. We must never forget this if we truly want to achieve new levels of personal productivity.

Apply the fitness of use definition by Dr. Juran. Accept the fact that if process participants and managers can't easily use what we give them, it is the designer's failure not theirs.

Make everything as simple as possible. For every hour, day and week we spend on simplifying process experiences the organization will recoup those investments in perpetuity.

We need to make process experiences as flexible as possible, recognizing that in the trenches a process is stalked daily by Murphy's Law.

Finally, keep in mind that less is more at every level of process interaction. We must make *everything* as simple as we possibly can, and that includes making the user experience highly intuitive.

Step Four – Orchestrate for Real-Time Demand
1. Recognize that "as hoc" is the Real World of Process.
2. Remember, Murphy's Law Thrives in Work.
3. Don't Design in Complex Orchestration.
4. Do Design in Flexibility.

5. Enable Variable-based Orchestration.
6. Enable Routing-based Orchestration.

For managers, the real world of process sometimes seems to be one long string of exceptions that constantly violate all of the rules of our processes. Orchestrating process for real-time demand requires us to design our processes with this reality in mind. The challenges are real and we must address them.

Unexpected process "adjustments" are the rule more than the exception

Murphy's Law thrives in process: *"If anything can go wrong, it will..."*

Murphy's Law states that anything that can go wrong, will go wrong. If we challenge our processes from this perspective, we are dealing with the reality of process. Suffice it to say that under this premise, the flexibility our processes will take on is far more likely to make those processes useful and usable.

Orchestration for real-time demand requires that we empower managers to change orchestration rules by changing limits, using different criteria and even complex expressions.

While we may not be able to do all of this, we should strive hard to take this concept as far as we can.

The result if we do this will have dramatic impacts on the organization. Work will often continue to flow smoothly even when the context around it is turbulent and unpredictable. The real challenge of process orchestration is not the 80% of the norm that we can build into the process model; it is the 20% of the exceptions that often burn through 80% of our work resources.

We need to include flexibility if and where we can, enabling managers to reorder activities or skip some altogether. It may not seem like we should, and in some cases we should not, but this is what happens in the real world. Either our processes are part of the problem or through real-time orchestration they are part of the solution.

Step Five – Keep your Process in Tune
1. Ensure that Reactive Tuning Measures are in Place.
2. Use Reactive Measures as a Baseline for Process Tuning.
3. Put Active Measures in Place against Goals.
4. Use Active Measures to Protect Gains and Improve Reaction times.
5. Identify Adaptive Measures.
6. Find Ways to Track Adaptive Measures.
7. Use Adaptive Measures to Identify Changes before they become Problems.

Processes, and the context they exist in, are constantly changing. They must be tuned to the current context if we expect them to serve their intended purpose.

Reactive measures are likely to be available for many processes. These include increases in processing time, the formation of bottlenecks, uncompleted work and increases in errors. Reactive measures are the common process characteristics that tell us when something has gone wrong.

Insuring that reactive measures are in place and that they are monitored is the first step in tuning processes. If we do nothing else, we must at least use reactive measures to periodically move our processes back to efficient operation,

Active measures stem from the KPIs we used for our goals in step one. We use these measures to protect process improvement gains and ensure that we retain business value. These KPIs are typically monitored on a periodic basic with an auditing schedule that is adjusted to our findings.

Adaptive tuning requires that we identify measures that capture actual working patterns. With adaptive measures we can proactively detect even subtle needs for process changes and take action before they encroach on improvement gains or business value. The challenge with adaptive changes is in identifying the measures we can use to detect work pattern changes. By looking for common or standard work patterns, we can identify data entry, document, form, task and other elements that form the patterns of how work gets done.

With these measures in place, we can create what is in effect an early warning system for our processes that gives us the insight and time to intelligently address process or context changes before they are able to grow in to problems.

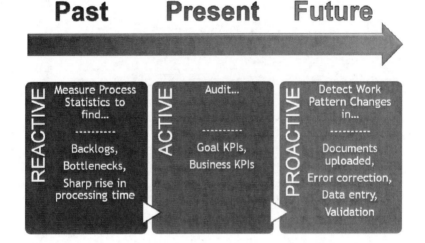

Step Six – Create Transparency
1. Use the Power of Rapid Cognition.
2. Understand the Hierarchy of Process Data.
>   By Activity
>   By Process
>   By Functional Area
>   By Enterprise
3. Roll up Data to Create Process Powered Transparency.
4. Break Down KPIs to Create Personal Analytics.

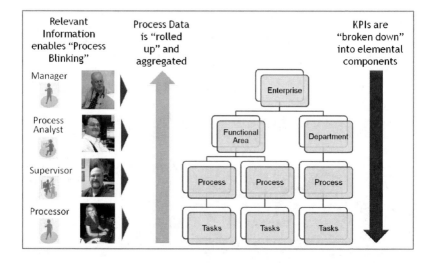

Transparency is not just about data or information, transparency is also about the *right* information presented in the *right* way for each of the different roles in the organization. We must enable rapid cognition wherever possible, as this will empower the organization to quickly make the right decisions, in the right way.

Rapid Cognition requires that we present the smallest data set of highly valuable information for the different decisions that managers make. By visually presenting these small but high value datasets in a visually intuitive manner we will trigger rapid cognition.

We do this by understanding the process data hierarchy. The hierarchy is based on the information we can collect and store at the task or activity level of the process. From there, we can begin rolling that data up, aggregating as we go.

This yields highly informative aggregate views of functional areas and for the entire enterprise. Each view is essential as the one before, with the caveat that the higher we go up the process hierarchy the more the aggregated data sits behind the view. In this way we are able to use existing process metrics to create relevant process views for each management role in the organization. However, to have true transparency we must also break high-level KPIs down through the process hierarchy. Here we are starting with the aggregate view and breaking it down to the relevant constituent sets of data that will create the relevant perspective on KPIs at each level.

When we bring these two powerful concepts together, along with the context of the high-level KPIs we can provide process managers and participants with personal analytics in context with the reasoning behind them.

Step Seven – Design, Manage and Deliver the Customer Experience

1. Map the Existing Customer Experience.
2. Define the Desired Customer Experience.
3. Create Customer Experience KPIs.
4. Optimize for Delivery.

The customer experience is an outside-in perspective on process. That perspective, which is the only perspective the customer cares about, is infrequently addressed in BPM projects, resulting in a disconnect between internal processes and the external customer experience.

Creating the connection between the customer experience and internal processes is a critical step that organizations must take, for the customer is any company's chief asset.

Making the connection starts by mapping the existing customer experience and identifying the moments of truth of the process the customer interacts with. Each customer interaction involves a Moment of Truth.

With the customer experience mapped, we can now challenge that experience and design the experience we want to deliver to our customers. From that definition of the desired customer experience we produce customer experience KPIs that we can use for measuring and managing delivery.

We can refine the process to achieve related KPIs and eliminate non value-added activities wherever they exist. Optimization of the customer experience often requires that we address multiple internal processes and functional areas. As with internal processes, the customer experience KPIs must be broken down to relevant sub-goals across the internal processes that sit behind it.

Where Do We Go From Here?

By Peter Fingar

The Road goes ever on and on
   Down from the door where it began.
Now far ahead the Road has gone,
   And I must follow, if I can,
Pursuing it with eager feet,
   Until it joins some larger way
Where many paths and errands meet.
   And whither then? I cannot say.
—Bilbo Baggins (J.R.R Tolkien)

It's been a fascinating journey full of twists and turns since 2002 and the release of the book, *Business Process Management: The Third Wave*, with its vision of BPM as a powerful new business asset. Here's a brief recap of that vision:

"BPM enables a pervasive, resilient, and predictable means for the processing of processes, a permanent business change laboratory, enabling ongoing innovation, transformation and agility. Such 'process processing' should not be confused with automation. Digital process models may have little to do with computers but a lot to do with business. While automation can be readily achieved with a raft of existing technologies, BPM has a wider meaning. Not only does it encompass the discovery, design, and deployment of business processes, but also the executive, administrative, and supervisory control over them to ensure that they remain compliant with business objectives for the delight of customers. Processes are the main intellectual property and competitive differentiator manifest in all business activity, and companies must treat them with a great degree of skill and care.

"For this to happen, processes must be explicit. In short, 'data processing' must give way to 'process processing.' Companies must obliterate the business-IT divide, transforming legacy into an asset rather than a liability. If this analysis seems extreme, consider the fact that every modern management theory ever devised – reengineering, process innovation, total quality management, Six Sigma, activity-based costing, value-chain analysis, cycle-time reduction, supply chain management, excellence, customer-driven strategy, and management by objectives – has stressed the significance of the business process and its management. In light of this constant demand, it seems surprising that the IT industry has up to now delivered only 'business applications.' Forget bridging the divide. Don't perfect IT with another layer of complexity, another silver bullet. We've been there and it doesn't work. Instead, place the emphasis where it belongs: Give ownership of business process management back to business people."

It probably won't surprise you to learn that BPM has traversed the proverbial hype curve, but with some unusual twists. By several measures, BPM, as set forth in the vision of The Third Wave, has hit, not the stage of disillusionment, but a cone of silence. Consider these talking points:

■ BPM conferences are lacking attendance.

It seems conference attendance is way down. Why is that? Perhaps it's due to a downturned economy? Perhaps due to BPM pure plays having gone through their initial marketing budgets and dropping sponsorship? And, the IT/BPM vendors, the big fish, swallow little fish, further reducing the sponsorships. After a recent conference in Chicago, a keynote speaker reported that he was underwhelmed, "mostly unempowered techies given a reward to go downtown." After another conference, an attendee reported, "Same old message, same 'ole speakers, new powerpoints." Frits Bussemaker of the BPM Forum stated that "Most conferences present a series of monologues, not the needed dialogs and collaborations." Ouch, is BPM dead?

■ Business process management has become
  IT process management.

Wasn't BPM supposed to be about empowering business people to take control of their processes? It seems, in actuality, that BPM suites are being used by IT people to develop IT applications. Has BPM been reduced to just another agile applications development method? Wasn't the original point that

BPM would provide full process lifecycle management – to business people? While The Third Wave described a new way to automate business processes, it's not only that. It is also a new mode of control over the process, comprising eight broad process capabilities: discovery, design, deployment, execution, interaction, control, optimization, and analysis (forever in a loop of improvement and re-design). The hallmark of the BPMS, therefore, is the combination of automation and design in one package. Why would anyone want it otherwise? As it turns out, instead of BPM being about process improvement and process innovation, so far many BPM initiatives have been about application development and application integration. Ouch, is BPM dead?

■ The BPM pure plays are in the shadows of
   IT platform vendors.

In "Sizing Up the BPM Leaders," industry analyst, Bruce Sliver, wrote, "When asked to name leaders in BPM software, more than 1,600 readers elevated only three names above the crowd: all three were major IT platform vendors that describe BPM as one possible flavor of agile application development based on their new service-oriented middleware stacks. That's disheartening to "pure play" BPM suite vendors, whose offerings not only provide more of the industry analysts' must-have functionality but also more closely adhere to their view of BPM's purpose: business performance optimization through modeling, human task automation and business activity monitoring (BAM). Somewhere between the analysts' picture of BPM and users' perceptions of technology leadership, there's a major disconnect." Ouch, is BPM dead?

■ The SOA push has obfuscated BPM.

With SOA developers as the primary target of the IT platform vendors, BPM is positioned as a niche, buried in an IT stack, when "orchestration" is needed. Surely, that's a small letter "bpm," and a useful tool for service-oriented applications development, but not the BPM that can transform companies and position them to compete in the brave new world of total global competition. With the focus of IT vendors' marketing campaigns on SOA, SOA is all the rage in the IT press, muffling the BPM as the three-letter acronym of the day. Ouch, is BPM dead?

■ Turfdoms are alive and well.

Deep-seated cultural issues rise to the surface when anyone or anything crosses boundaries in an organization. Long-time management coach and BPM expert Andrew Spanyi wrote at length about the cultural barriers to becoming a process-managed enterprise in both his books, BPM is a Team Sport, and More for Less. But more than words in books, Spanyi observes these very same issues in the trenches during his consulting engagements. Perhaps these issues can be compared to those uncovered in applying management techniques such as Lean that were developed in Asian cultures and were difficult to transplant to Western cultures. At heart are social philosophies of collectivism, where group goals take priority over individual goals, versus individualism where the exercise of one's goals opposes any external interference. It's all about what kind of company a firm wants to be and the kind of culture needed for that kind of company. Command and control leadership gives way to connect and collaborate in a process-managed enterprise where every member of a business team is a "leader." In a process-managed enterprise, leaders don't give commands, they transmit information, trusting the team members' competencies and gaining accountability through transparency. True leadership is about cooperation, not control. It's about acting on opportunities, and letting others lead the leader when they know best about getting stuff done. It's clear that transforming a company to a process-managed enterprise is first and foremost about cultural issues, and this has no doubt been an obstacle to BPM adoption in many organizations. Grown people are set in their ways, hard to change, and don't want to give up their status (just carry on with the same old, same old ... until the end). Bussemaker adds, "BPM makes an organization very transparent so, you cannot hide your mistakes anymore." Ouch, is BPM dead?

- BPM implementations have largely been tactical,
  not strategic.

  Although there's been great progress in the theory of BPM, deployments have so far been mostly tactical and limited in scope, applying to improvements in specific business functions and departments. Tactical BPM only offers a way of improving what a company already does (paving cow paths). BPM's full potential offers a strategic capability for achieving breakout competitive advantage through process innovation as well as incremental process improvements – a company needs many small wins and an occasional home run to win at the game of extreme competition. The scope and complexity increases exponentially as companies progress from tactical point-solution BPM to enterprise BPM where cross-functional processes are taken on, and on to value-chain BPM where totally new cross-company processes emerge and must be managed. To meet these needs, raw BPM capability isn't enough – that's the blank screen syndrome. Opening a screen on a newly installed BPM suite should reveal industry specific templates and frameworks such as the Value Chain Group's reference model that can help companies reach across the entire value delivery system. Frankly, even the early adopters of BPM aren't there yet and will need to continue to climb the BPM maturity ladder. But the effort must be made, for today competition is about setting the pace of innovation in an industry – across the entire value chain. It's about forming new multi-company alliances (sometimes even with competitors) to innovate new value delivery systems that span a firm's suppliers' suppliers and its customers' customers. This is the stuff of strategic deployments of BPM, and it's something no company can do alone. If companies cannot grow beyond back-office tactical BPM, then BPM will be relegated to being just another application development and integration tool. Ouch, is BPM dead?

■ Process modeling is still done on the walls of caves.

Have companies really evolved beyond the pictograms of our ancestors? Of course, everybody in the BPM kingdom knows about BPMN and its virtues. But what's the number one process pictogram tool of choice to this day? BPMN, ARIS, or UML? None of the above. It's Visio. Right now it's Visio over the wall to IT. If we are going to connect the caves to build new business ecosystems for the 21st century, we've got to scratch our collective heads and think of pictograms all can understand – and use. Business people don't take naturally to detailed transaction-oriented process modeling, and are too busy to become fully trained on complex modeling tools, even if they have the aptitude. Because process discovery and modeling are the cornerstones for understanding what a company really does and the foundation for understanding both automated and human business processes, unless related tools and techniques are greatly simplified and made business-people friendly, a company isn't even going to get off the BPM starting block. Ouch, is BPM dead?

This list of talking points could no doubt go on, but enough said already. So, there you have it. BPM is dead, at least as envisioned by the pioneers who saw a future where the business people regained control of their business processes that were locked away in complex, hard-coded enterprise systems that required tedious rewiring for even the slightest process change.

Oh well, BPM was, at least, a really good idea.

But Wait!

Actually, the downturn in BPM conference attendance could indeed be a good sign. As one practitioner and regular conference attendee reported, "We are now staying home doing the work, and spending most of our education and training budget on specific training. We 'got it,' and now are doing it." In the current downturn, companies are indeed tightening conference budgets, but they are also desperately seeking performance improvements and adjustments to the current economic realities. The ability to handle process change isn't always in response to new growth opportunities; it's needed to revise business operations during downturns as well. In a world where getting work done depends on computers, companies want to know how they can rise to the challenges they face, right now. And that's precisely where BPM capabilities fit in, in good times and bad, in the "fierce urgency of now." Companies are now going beyond conference messages of "what and why BPM" and seeking "how to actually do BPM." So while conference attendance may be down, the demand for hands-on, how-to trainers such as John Jeston, BPTrends Associates,

Bruce Silver, Derek Miers, and the service organizations of BPM vendors is growing.

Okay, BPM has become a technical sale from IT vendors to IT staffs, and SOA is all-the-buzz. But wait. SOA is not a concrete thing; it's architecture, it's a set of principles and design guidelines. And, yes, such architecture can be extremely helpful in harnessing the potential of BPM across companies and across value chains, but BPM, as both a management approach and a technology, is orthogonal to SOA. SOA doesn't replace BPM; it's an enabler that can give BPM reach. BPM suites would best be built from the ground up based on SOA – Call this approach SOA BPM if you like. SOA is the next big thing in the evolution of software engineering disciplines, but don't confuse SOA as the next big thing superseding BPM. SOA doesn't need BPM, and BPM doesn't need SOA. But, together they are a winning combination to bring sorely needed process management capabilities to the entire value chain.

We will, no doubt, have to wait years for the cultural shift toward a fully process-managed enterprise. Or will we? Let's turn to the closing of Andrew Spanyi's BPM is a Team Sport, "Those who fail to transform the traditional functional mindset and embrace business process thinking will find themselves teetering on the brink. Indeed, BPM is a highly competitive team sport, and in the playoffs for industry championships, it's win or be eliminated." The days of the monolithic, vertically integrated company, owning everything from raw materials to production to selling, are over. 21st-century corporations will thrive in a business world where the traditional linear supply chain gives way to dynamic, customer-driven value webs (call it the extended enterprise if you like). Pain is indeed a great motivator and globalization is the greatest reorganization of the world since the Industrial Revolution, bringing great pain to those who hold on to yesteryear's business models in today's wired world. Industries will be disrupted either by new entrants or by incumbents that move from command and control to connect-and-collaborate leadership for process innovation that spans entire value chains. To wit, consider what Amazon did to the retail book industry and what Dell did to the PC industry. Thus, the cultural shift to a processed-managed enterprise as a management practice may come a lot sooner than some may think, and at the expense of inflexible business leaders and their companies.

But wait, what exactly does "management practice" actually mean? Let's turn to John Jeston's book, *Beyond Business Process Improvement, On To Business Transformation*: "The first step in discussing BPM is to ensure that we have a common understanding and agreement that BPM is a management philosophy. Yes, it is also about completing business process improvement projects to make your processes more efficient and effective (thirty to fifty percent is normal). Yes, it is about then continuing to measure and performance manage the processes into the future. But it is much more than just this. Just making your business processes more efficient and effective does not mean your organization will be managed better, as process performance advantages will dissipate over time. More is required.

"BPM is a management 'tool' or philosophy that will enable an organization to significantly improve its performance. It will enable managers to become high performance managers, and if you have enough high performance managers, you are well on the way to being a high performance organization.

"In looking at our business processes, we need to go beyond the normal process thinking. Business processes are not just about the 'transactional' processes we traditionally think about. Transactional processes are those that process your cash receipts; insurance premiums; bank withdrawals; order fulfillment. But, business processes also include: organizational strategy creation and review; budget processes; management decision making; capital allocation; and internal communications. These are the processes that govern the work that gets done by the transactional processes.

"Organizations need to continually review, improve or eliminate these management processes as much or more than the 'traditional' customer-serving processes. Management processes often need more attention because most have not been reviewed for a long time and as observed by renowned management professor, Gary Hamel, 'they shape management values by reinforcing certain behaviors and not others.'"

Current flavors of workflow and integration style BPM technology have a long way to go before we'll see the implementation of the holistic BPMS envisioned in The Third Wave. Along the way, BPM Suites, currently composed of federations of workflow, EAI and rules technologies will likely evolve into the comprehensive technology of the BPMS that embeds the computer science of mathematically underpinned mobile processes, where computation and communication fuse as one. Here's more from The Third Wave:

"The essence of the BPM innovation is that we now understand data, procedure, workflow, and distributed communication not as apples, oranges, and cherries, but as one new business 'information type' (what technologists call an 'abstract data type') – the business process. The recognition of this new fundamental building block is profound, for each element in a complete business process (the inputs, the outputs, the participants, the activities, and the calculations) can now be expressed in a form where every facet and feature can be understood in the context of its use, its purpose, and its role in decision making. This problem-solving paradigm can therefore provide a single basis not only to express any process, but as the basis for a wide variety of process management systems and process-aware tools and services."

Like simulation, to date there has been no screaming demand for the underlying sophistication of mobile processes whose components communicate and change their structure in flight. But, as companies climb the BPM maturity ladder and begin to reach across the value chain with human interaction management and knowledge-centered processes, watch for the rebirth of The Third Wave BPMS and the growing use of mobile process underpinnings in service-oriented computing.

CSC's Howard Smith made the point, "We had to wait years for the development of mature technologies that can directly model, manage, and execute business processes – for the realization of a unified, holistic business process-centric approach. Mature full-featured data management (RDBMS) products took twenty years to mature. Why should BPMS be any different?"

For the moment, BPM vendors will likely continue to focus their sales efforts at IT departments. But that's not all bad, for companies' some IT professionals such as Information Architects transcend silos and departmental boundaries to have the broadest perspective of a company from a systems theory point of view. I've written before that as the business world moves beyond the tinkering phase with tactical BPM point solutions and on to multi-enterprise process management for true process and value-chain innovation, complexity will explode. Thus BPM, the next generation, will require the complexity buster of The Third Wave BPMS, incorporating process-oriented architecture and methods, human interaction management, complex event processing, and agent technology. No, this isn't some mad computer scientist's dream; it's what's required by the messy and complex real world of business. All this will take true IT leadership, but not the kind of technical IT leadership of the past.

Contemplating any company's push for operational innovation, the implications for IT professionals are profound. Companies don't want more IT; they want business results. If companies are to embrace Operational Transformation, they will need a far greater contribution from IT than ever before, but that contribution will be of a substantially different nature. For Operational Transformation to come about, a system-wide view of the company is needed, and some IT professionals have such a view, far more than the marketing, legal, financial, and other specialists in the firm. Building the process-managed, real-time enterprise will demand innovation and rigorous systems thinking from a new generation of IT professionals, stressing some to their limits as the process paradigm shift takes hold. It's not your father's IT shop any more, and business process management skills now outweigh yesterday's technical skills. The forward thinking CIO will no doubt evolve to become the CPO, Chief Process Officer, for it's agile business processes that companies want to manage, not technology infrastructures. IT leadership will evolve to become business leadership, for business is indeed a complex system requiring a mastery of general systems thinking that can be used to manage business processes built not to last, but built to compete, built for setting the pace of innovation.. So, instead of the simple notion that BPM technology should be "sold" to business units, targeting IT units in a company will likely be the way that BPM seeds are planted in the larger business organization, via the business-savvy CIO or CPO as emissary. Some of today's CIOs, especially those who climbed the ranks in business units, are indeed as business savvy as they are technology savvy. They understand business processes embedded in information systems across the entire organization. Technical IT staff that chooses not to become deeply involved in process management, and morph into process analysts instead of IT analysts, will likely be delegated to maintaining the technology much as the building maintenance staff attends to the air conditioning systems. Meanwhile, the CIO/CPO will likely toil away in the executive suite where life and death business decisions must be made and business strategies formulated and executed. It's no doubt time to have business drive IT change instead of IT determining the pace of business change – and new process management roles and responsibilities will drive the transformation.

The ability to anticipate and deal with growing complexity is essential in the brave new world of global competition, and process modeling and analysis tools also need to better accommodate business people so they can more fully participate in all stages of process lifecycle management. Generation Z, now moving into their careers in business, will accept nothing less than Web 2.0 simplicity – in their personal interactions – and in their process modeling and management tools. Repeating that which I've written before, the shift to Web 2.0 has come about largely by the simplicity of use – Call it Consumer IT, if you will. You don't need to write even one line of code to participate in Facebook, YouTube, MySpace, Second Life, Wikis, blogs, or Google Apps. This then leads to the question, "Why is Consumer IT so simple and Enterprise IT so complex?" Answering this question unfolds many challenges and opportunities for the worlds of IT and BPM. More and more, business people will turn to organic Web 2.0 document and task-centric workflow tools that embody the simplicity of Consumer IT. Such tools are typically purchased or used for free by individuals or work groups completely outside the purview of their IT department. Such tools are generally browser based (think SaaS), and don't require in-house IT resources. This megatrend will no doubt shape the form and function of today's complex process modeling and process change tools. Web 2.0 accommodates complexity without requiring end users to understand the underlying technology to put it to use. But keep in mind that simple to use doesn't mean simple systems; quite the contrary. Under the covers, Web 2.0 technology is highly complex --yes, easy to use, but difficult to leverage effectively. Don't be surprised to know that forward-looking BPM vendors are hard at work simplifying their tools to open them to a new breed of ambidextrous business power users – There aren't enough programmers in the world to do otherwise. Advanced business rules capabilities and SOA governance will keep mayhem from breaking out as more and more business power users take the helm of business process change. Veteran business architect, Gene Weng, netted it out with a quote from Leonardo da Vinci, "Simplicity is the ultimate sophistication."

No doubt the original Third Wave vision of BPM will be "born again." Call it BPM 2.0 or BPM 15.0, SOA-BPM, or Mobile Process Management. Or, from a business perspective call it Business Operations Management (BOM 2.0 anyone?), because it's no longer what you do, it's how you do what you do, how you operate your business, that counts – and that's about operational innovation, and that, in turn, is about business process innovation. Call it what you like, the growing complexity of the global economy, where no company is an island, will demand business process management capabilities powered by a business operations platform that has Third Wave BPM technology at its heart.

BPM is dead – Baloney! Okay, maybe it's currently a little comatose. But, quite frankly, businesses don't give a hoot about any three-letter acronym, including BPM, save one: ROI. And ROI is all about managing change to rise to the challenge of an increasingly complex world of Extreme Competition; which; in turn, is about adroit process management.

The Last Word – Process Excellence

To close out this book we turn to an interview conducted by *Business Pioneer* magazine. The magazine is a leading business publication in the countries of the Gulf Cooperation Council (GCC) that include Bahrain, Kuwait, Oman, Qatar, Saudi Arabia and the United Arab Emirates. Though recognized leaders of the hydrocarbon economy, the GCC countries are determined to be world-class leaders in the process-driven economy. The lessons they are learning in their transformation apply globally, just as the lessons of quality learned by the Japanese after WWII have been applied across the industrial world. The interview was on the subject of Process Excellence.

Business Pioneer: Business process excellence seems to be an important topic on corporate agendas. What is really meant by business process excellence?

Terry: It certainly is a hot topic on most corporate agendas. Business process excellence is concerned with several things. Foremost is reducing costs without impacting service quality. Of course everyone is concerned about reducing costs, but process excellence reduces costs by improving both the efficiency and quality of business processes. This is much different from the cost-cutting practices of the past.

Business Pioneer: You said business process excellence is concerned with several things. What else besides cost is it concerned with?

Terry: Value. More importantly, customer value creation and competitive differentiation. No matter where we are in the world these days the business competition is fierce. More and more businesses are realizing they have to differentiate in a way that creates customer loyalty. The economics just aren't there any more for continued high customer acquisition costs unless we are able to keep those new customers we acquire.

Business Pioneer: It certainly is a competitive business world. But how does process excellence create customer value and customer loyalty?

Terry: This is one of the most important insights we have finally brought into perspective. Virtually all interactions are processes. Customer interactions are certainly processes. Recognizing this, we are now starting to take clear ownership over these customer processes because they are the only processes the customer really cares about. When business process excellence includes those customer processes – which more and more organizations are now doing – those processes are designed, optimized and managed for the express purpose of creating customer satisfaction. This is a powerful way to build customer loyalty and gain the advantage of positive word of mouth advertising (which is free).

Business Pioneer: So business process excellence is not just about improving efficiency and quality of work, it is also about improving customer processes. Is that correct?

Terry: Absolutely. While improving our internal processes is certainly valuable, the big wins come when we address both customer processes and internal processes. When companies get this right they always realize three benefits: decreased cost, enhanced customer satisfaction and increased revenues.

Business Pioneer: How have the economic challenges affected the pursuit of business process excellence?

Terry: Most people are experiencing significant pressure from the economic turbulence and uncertainty we have now. Because of that we are seeing more solid progress on achieving real gains in process improvement. Our focus is sharper and we are working harder to produce great results as a response to this pressure and uncertainty. The result is that we are seeing more notable achievements in the pursuit of business process excellence than we have ever seen before.

Business Pioneer: Is everyone focusing on business process excellence? Has it become the way organizations are meeting the economic challenges?

Terry: No. Some businesses are simply reducing all expenditures that they can and then waiting for things to get better. They are aggressively managing their financials and little else.

Business Pioneer: Will that work?

Terry: That depends. There are some industries and geographies that businesses can get away with that but it is risky. I mean, when economies stabilize again we will see a strong out flow of spending. In most cases I think that the businesses that are busy fine-tuning every aspect of their business by pursing business process excellence will be in a great position to capitalize on that out flow. Many of their competitors who have just taken cover and waited out the storm are likely to find themselves in a poor competitive position then.

Business Pioneer: What about the Middle East? Does business process excellence have any special importance here?

Terry: It certainly does. The ongoing expansion of far greater business diversity in the Middle East than existed in the past makes business process excellence a critical initiative to the region. When we think about it, the opportunity is to diversify with the ideal end result being economic independence. But to achieve that you have to diversify and be competitive on the world scene at the same time. That is not an easy thing to do. Business excellence is a very big part of the answer.

Business Pioneer: Where do you think the Middle East is on the subject of business process excellence compared to other countries?

Terry: That is a great question. I would best characterize the Middle East as being behind while in the "process" of becoming a leader. While other parts of the world have been employing some of the aspects of business process excellence longer than in the Middle East they are not as dedicated and focused as what I'm seeing in the region now. Though the comparison is only a general one, it is kind of like the quality initiatives that came out of the United States lead by Deming and Juran that were adopted far more aggressively by Japan resulting in their very rapid rise as a manufacturing power on the world scene. I would not be surprised to see a similar kind of result in the Middle East. But the change here will consist of less and less market success from companies outside the region with more and more export success from within the region. That is an ideal case of economic health and vitality.

Business Pioneer: Thank you for taking the time to speak with us today.

References

[1] *Reengineering the Corporation: A Manifesto for Business Revolution* by Michael Hammer and James Champy

[2] *Business Process Management: The Third Wave* by Howard Smith and Peter Fingar

[3] *BPM Pulse Survey 2009* by BPM Partners (www.bpmpartners.com)

[4] *A Survey of Business Process Initiatives 2007* by Nathaniel Palmer published by BPTrends

[5] Gartner Technology Business Research

[6] Aberdeen Group

[7] Dr. William Edwards Deming

[8] Dr. Joseph M. Juran

[9] *On Intelligence* by Jeff Hawkins

[10] zur Muehlen, M., Recker, J. (2008): How Much Language is Enough? Theoretical and Practical Use of the Business Process Modeling Notation. In Z. Bellahsene and M. Leonard (eds.): Advanced Information Systems Engineering - CAiSE 2008. Lecture Notes in Computer Science, Volume 5074. Springer, Montpellier, France, pp. 465-479. Copyright Springer-Verlag.

[11] *Nonfarm Business Sector Productivity* by US Bureau of Labor Statistics

[12] *The Design of Everyday Things* by Donald A Norman

[13] *Reference Guide on our Freedom & Responsibility Culture* by Reed

Hastings, NefFlix CEO as posted on Slideshare (www.slideshare.com)

[14] Mike Abramsky, analyst with RBC Capital Markets

[15] *Blink: The Power of Thinking Without Thinking* by Malcolm Gladwell

[16] *Customer Expectation Management: Success Without Exception* by Terry Schurter

[17] *The Legend of Discount Tire* by Jeffery L. Rodengen & Richard F. Hubbard

[18] Moments of Truth concept, Richard Norman

[19] *Moments of Truth: New Strategies for Today's Customer-Driven Economy* by Jan Carlzon

[20] *The Tipping Point: How Little Things Can Make a Big Difference* by Malcolm Gladwell

Index

About the Author

TERRY SCHURTER is an internationally recognized process expert, receiving the Global Thought Leadership Award in 2007 from the BPM Group. He currently serves as Director of Product Strategy for Global360 and is Chairman of the Board of Advisors for the International Process and Performance Institute. He has held executive positions including CEO, CIO, VP of Strategy and VP of Engineering. In his 25 years experience in business management he has held senior management positions at Bloor Research, Bennu Group, 3Rings Technologies, Eon Mobility, USDATA, xFactory, and Westinghouse, where he won the prestigious George Westinghouse Signature of Excellence award two years in a row. He is an international speaker (including Fortune 50 C-level events), a Certified Process Professional Coach, and is an author of five books including *Customer Expectation Management: Success Without Exception*, cited as a manifesto for customer focused companies; *Technologies for Government Transformation: ERP Systems and Beyond*, awarded the 2006 Award for Most Effective Education by the Government Research Association and named to the Top Ten Books for Public CIOs by Public CIO Magazine; and *In Search of BPM Excellence*.

Contributor, **PETER FINGAR** is an internationally recognized expert on business strategy and business process management. He's a former CIO and practitioner with over thirty years of hands-on experience at the intersection of business and technology. He has held management, technical and advisory positions with GTE Data Services, American Software and Computer Services, Saudi Aramco, EC Cubed, the Technical Resource Connection division of Perot Systems, and IBM Global Services. He has taught graduate and undergraduate computing studies at business schools in the U.S. and abroad, and gives keynote talks worldwide. He is an author of nine books, including the landmark books *Dot.Cloud: The 21st Century Business Platform; Extreme Competition; The Real-Time Enterprise;* and *Business Process Management: The Third Wave.* His current writings can be found at www.PeterFingar.com.

Your Complete BPM Library
Innovation at the Intersection of Business and Technology
www.mkpress.com